quick-method
QUILTS
GALORE

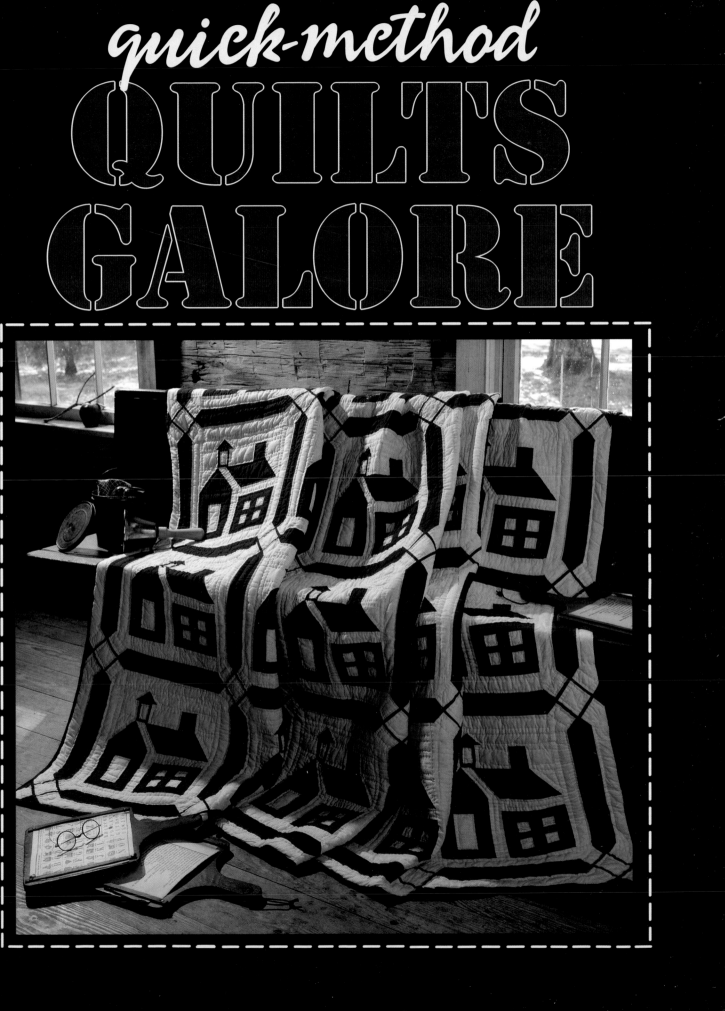

EDITORIAL STAFF

Vice President and Editor-in-Chief:
Anne Van Wagner Childs
Executive Director: Sandra Graham Case
Executive Editor: Susan Frantz Wiles
Publications Director: Carla Bentley
Creative Art Director: Gloria Bearden
Production Art Director: Melinda Stout

DESIGN
Design Director: Patricia Wallenfang
Sowers
Senior Designer: Linda Diehl Tiano

PRODUCTION
Managing Editor: Sherry Taylor O'Connor
Technical Writers: Sherry Solida Ford,
Kathleen Coughran Magee, and Barbara
McClintock Vechik

EDITORIAL
Associate Editor: Linda L. Trimble
Senior Editorial Writer: Terri Leming
Davidson
Editorial Associates: Tammi Williamson
Bradley and Robyn Sheffield-Edwards
Copy Editor: Laura Lee Weland

ART
Book/Magazine Art Director: Diane M.
Ghegan
Senior Production Artist: M. Katherine
Yancey
Art Production Assistants: Rhonda Shelby
and Brent Jones
Photography Stylists: Christina Tiano
Myers and Karen Smart Hall

BUSINESS STAFF

Publisher: Bruce Akin
Vice President, Finance: Tom Siebenmorgen
Vice President, Retail Sales: Thomas L.
Carlisle
Retail Sales Director: Richard Tignor
Vice President, Retail Marketing: Pam
Stebbins
Retail Customer Services Director:
Margaret Sweetin

Marketing Manager: Russ Barnett
**Executive Director of Marketing and
Circulation:** Guy A. Crossley
Circulation Manager: Byron L. Taylor
Print Production Manager: Laura Lockhart
Print Production Coordinator: Nancy
Reddick Lister

Library of Congress Catalog Number 94-74354
Hardcover ISBN 0-942237-56-0
Softcover ISBN 0-942237-57-9

INTRODUCTION

From Grandma's favorite patterns to our original designs, you'll find the perfect quilt for your busy life in Quick-Method Quilts Galore. Flip through the pages and you'll admire all the different looks you can achieve — whether feminine, rustic, or classic — using the best of our time-saving hints. We're constantly developing handy shortcuts to update traditional quilting methods with the newest tools and techniques. Our tips even make it easier to work with templates and appliqués! In addition to taking a simplified approach, we rate the skill levels of our quilts, so you'll have no trouble selecting a project that's just right for you. If your schedule doesn't allow time for making a full-size quilt, you can still enjoy our patterns in a variety of smaller, faster projects, including a lap quilt, wall hangings, pillows, and decorated clothing. Whether you're a novice or an experienced quilter, this invaluable guide will help you make the most of your quilting moments!

TABLE OF CONTENTS

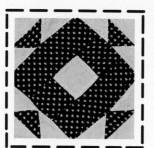

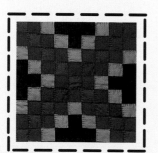

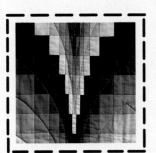
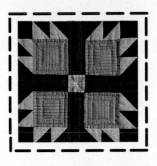

OHIO STAR

An ancient motif found in early Roman mosaics and Renaissance architecture, this simple star is one of the oldest patchwork patterns known. English quilters brought the design to America, and as pioneers settled along the Ohio River, it was named the Ohio Star in honor of their new home. This red and white beauty can be fashioned in a twinkling by cutting and re-assembling triangle-squares to create the stars' points. It's much easier and more accurate than traditional piecing! Finished with a lovely scalloped edging, the quilt is enhanced with basic grid and outline quilting.

OHIO STAR QUILT

SKILL LEVEL: 1 2 3 4 5
BLOCK SIZE: 8¼" x 8¼"
QUILT SIZE: 86" x 96"

YARDAGE REQUIREMENTS

Yardage is based on 45"w fabric.

☐ 8¼ yds of white solid

■ 2⅝ yds of red print
7½ yds for backing
1 yd for binding
120" x 120" batting

CUTTING OUT THE PIECES

All measurements include a ¼" seam allowance. Follow Rotary Cutting, page 144, to cut fabric.

1. **From white solid:**
   - Cut 16 selvage-to-selvage strips 8¾"w. From these strips, cut 62 **setting squares** 8¾" x 8¾".
   - Cut 19 selvage-to-selvage strips 3¼"w. From these strips, cut 224 **squares** 3¼" x 3¼".
   - Cut 2 squares 13" x 13". Cut squares twice diagonally to make 8 **setting triangles** (you will need 6 and have 2 left over).

square (cut 2)   **setting triangle** (cut 8)

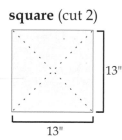

13" 13"

   - Cut 2 squares 6¾" x 6¾". Cut squares once diagonally to make 4 **corner setting triangles**.

square (cut 2)   **corner setting triangle** (cut 4)

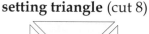

6¾" 6¾"

   - Cut 3 selvage-to-selvage strips 22"w. From these strips, cut 6 **rectangles** 18" x 22" for triangle-squares.

2. **From red print:** ■
   - Cut 5 selvage-to-selvage strips 3¼"w. From these strips, cut 56 **squares** 3¼" x 3¼".
   - Cut 3 selvage-to-selvage strips 22"w. From these strips, cut 6 **rectangles** 18" x 22" for triangle-squares.

ASSEMBLING THE QUILT TOP

Follow Piecing and Pressing, page 146, to make quilt top.

1. To make triangle-squares, place 1 red and 1 white **rectangle** right sides together. Referring to **Fig. 1**, follow Steps 1 - 3 of **Making Triangle-Squares**, page 147, to draw a grid of 20 squares 4" x 4". Referring to **Fig. 2** for stitching direction, follow Steps 4 - 6 of **Making Triangle-Squares** to complete 40 **triangle-squares**. Repeat with remaining **rectangles** to make a total of 240 **triangle-squares** (you will need 224 and have 16 left over).

Fig. 1

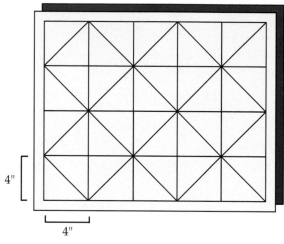

4"

4"

Fig. 2

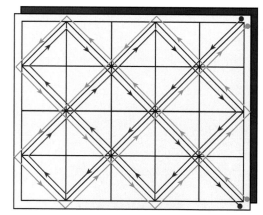

triangle-square (make 240)

2. Referring to **Fig. 3**, place 2 **triangle-squares** right sides and opposite colors together, matching seams. Referring to **Fig. 4**, mark a diagonal line from corner to corner. Stitch 1/4" on both sides of marked line. Cut apart on marked line and press open to make 2 **triangle units**. Repeat with remaining **triangle-squares** to make a total of 224 **triangle units**.

Fig. 3   **Fig. 4**

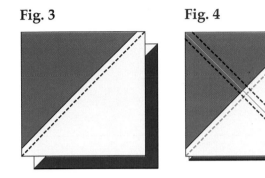

triangle unit (make 224)

3. Assemble 4 **triangle units** and 5 **squares** to make **Block**. Make 56 **Blocks**.

Block (make 56)

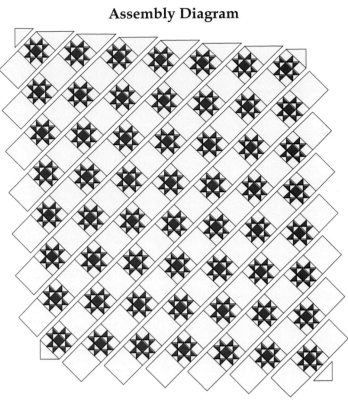

Assembly Diagram

4. Referring to **Assembly Diagram**, assemble **Blocks**, **setting squares**, **corner setting triangles**, and **setting triangles** into rows. Assemble rows to complete **Quilt Top**.

COMPLETING THE QUILT

1. Use **Scallop** pattern, page 13, and follow Step 2 of **Template Cutting**, page 146, to make scallop template. Referring to **Fig. 5**, mark a freehand curve on each **corner setting triangle** and use template to mark scallops on outer **setting squares**. Do not trim.

Fig. 5

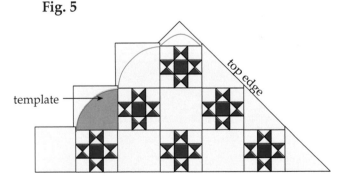

2. Follow **Quilting**, page 152, to mark, layer, and quilt, using **Quilting Diagram**, page 13, as a suggestion. Our quilt is hand quilted.
3. To prepare quilt for binding, use a narrow zigzag stitch with a medium stitch length to stitch along top raw edge of quilt top and just outside lines marked in Step 1.

11

4. Trim quilt top only to ¼" from marked line (**Fig. 6**).

Fig. 6

5. Cut a 32" square of binding fabric. Follow **Binding**, page 155, to make 2"w bias binding. To attach binding, follow Steps 1 and 2 of **Attaching Binding with Mitered Corners**, page 156, to pin binding to front of quilt. Easing binding around curves, sew binding to quilt, leaving a 2" overlap. Trim off excess binding and stitch overlap in place. Trim off excess batting and backing even with edge of quilt top. Fold binding over to quilt backing and pin in place, covering stitching line. Blindstitch binding to quilt backing.

Quilt Top Diagram

Quilting Diagram

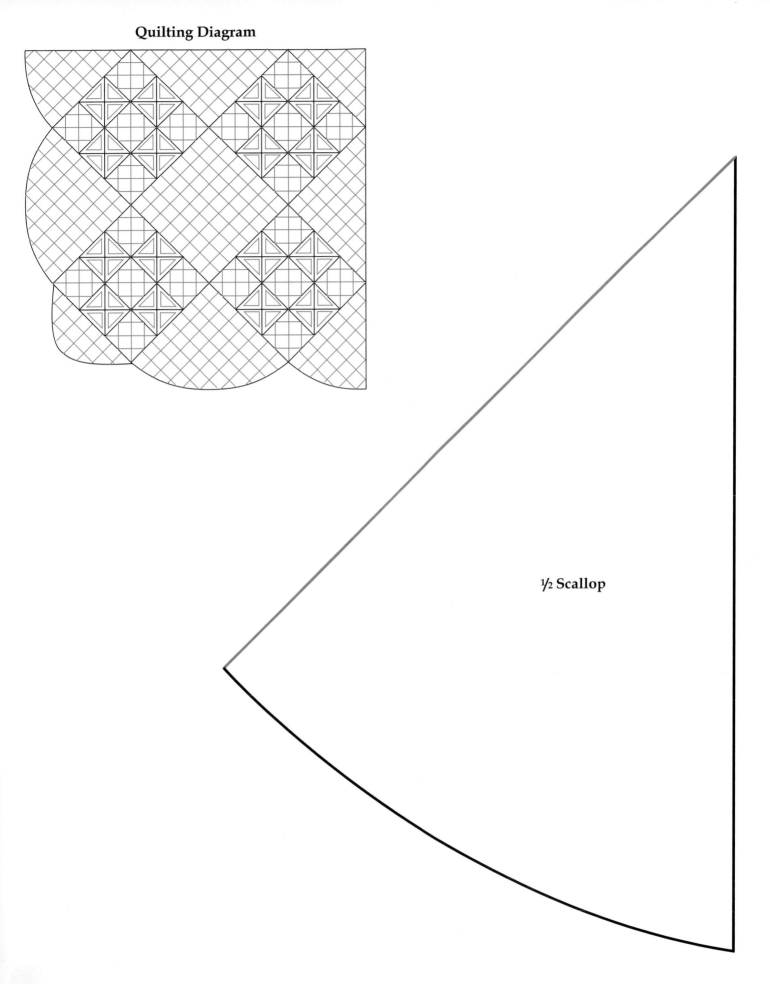

½ Scallop

ZIGZAG QUILT

Its bold pattern of contrasting triangles may look quite contemporary, but the Zigzag design actually dates back to the late nineteenth century. Stretching across the width of the quilt, the pattern was sometimes called Rail Fence because it resembled the rough-hewn barriers that bordered pioneer homesteads. When arranged vertically, however, it was known as Streak of Lightning. Our striking quilt is easy to assemble using large grid-pieced triangle-squares. Subtle texture is added with simple Baptist fan quilting.

ZIGZAG QUILT

SKILL LEVEL: 1 2 3 4 5
QUILT SIZE: 83" x 92"

YARDAGE REQUIREMENTS

Yardage is based on 45"w fabric.

 3¾ yds of blue solid

3⅜ yds of red solid

3⅜ yds of tan solid
7⅝ yds for backing
¾ yd for binding
90" x 108" batting

CUTTING OUT THE PIECES

All measurements include a ¼" seam allowance. Follow Rotary Cutting, page 144, to cut fabric.

1. **From blue solid:**
   - Cut 13 selvage-to-selvage strips 7"w. From these strips, cut 20 **rectangles** 7" x 20" and 16 **squares** 7" x 7".
   - Cut 1 square 10⅛" x 10⅛". Cut square once diagonally to make 2 **corner triangles**.

square (cut 1)   **corner triangle** (cut 2)

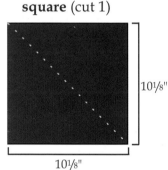

10⅛"

10⅛"

   - Cut 2 squares 19⅝" x 19⅝". Cut squares twice diagonally to make 8 **setting triangles**.

square (cut 2)   **setting triangle** (cut 8)

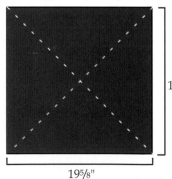
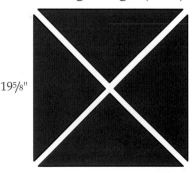

19⅝"

19⅝"

2. **From red solid:**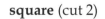
   - Cut 5 selvage-to-selvage strips 22"w. From these strips, cut 10 **rectangles** 18" x 22" for triangle-squares.

3. **From tan solid:**
   - Cut 5 selvage-to-selvage strips 22"w. From these strips, cut 10 **rectangles** 18" x 22" for triangle-squares.

ASSEMBLING THE QUILT TOP

Follow Piecing and Pressing, page 146, to make quilt top.

1. To make triangle-squares, place 1 red and 1 tan **rectangle** right sides together. Referring to **Fig. 1**, follow Steps 1 - 3 of **Making Triangle-Squares**, page 147, to draw a grid of 20 squares 4⅛" x 4⅛". Referring to **Fig. 2** for stitching direction, follow Steps 4 - 6 of **Making Triangle-Squares** to complete 40 triangle-squares. Repeat with remaining red and tan **rectangles** to make a total of 400 **triangle-squares** (you will need 380 and have 20 left over).

Fig. 1

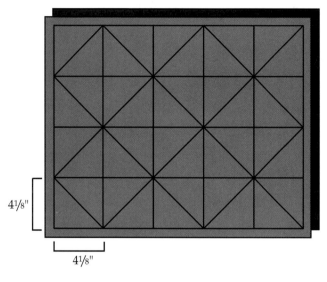

4⅛"

4⅛"

Fig. 2

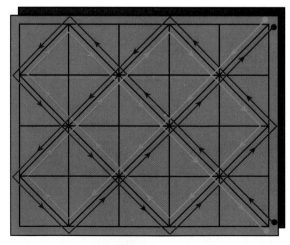

triangle-square (make 400)

2. Assemble 12 **triangle-squares** to make **Unit 1**. Make 25 **Unit 1's**. Assemble 4 **triangle-squares** to make **Unit 2**. Make 20 **Unit 2's**.

3. Referring to **Assembly Diagram**, assemble **Unit 1's** and **squares** into rows. Assemble **rectangles** and **Unit 2's** into rows. Assemble **corner triangles**, rows, and **setting triangles** to make quilt top.

Unit 1 (make 25)

Unit 2 (make 20)

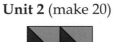

Assembly Diagram

17

4. Referring to **Fig. 3**, place ruler on quilt top with 1 long edge of ruler lined up with raw edge of 1 **corner triangle** and with ¼" marking (shown in pink) lined up with seam intersections. Trim off excess ends of **Unit 1's** and **rectangles** to complete **Quilt Top**.

Fig. 3

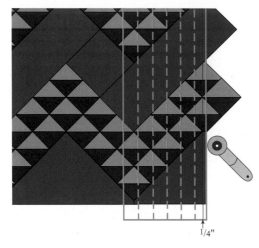

1/4"

COMPLETING THE QUILT

1. Follow **Quilting**, page 152, to mark, layer, and quilt, using **Quilting Diagram** as a suggestion. Our quilt is hand quilted with an all-over Baptist fan design.

2. Follow **Binding**, page 155, to bind quilt using 2½"w straight-grain binding with overlapped corners.

Quilting Diagram

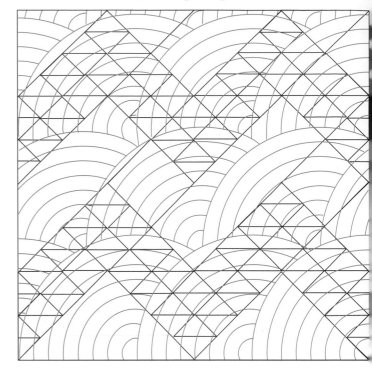

QUICK TIP

"AGING" NEW QUILTS

Part of the charm of old quilts is their wrinkled appearance and time-softened colors, not to mention the lovely prints that can bring back memories of our grandmothers. You can re-create that nostalgic look in the quick-method quilts you make today by using one or all of the following suggestions.

- *Use new fabrics that look like old fabrics! The reproduction prints that many fabric companies now carry have brought back some of the best colors and prints from the 1920's, 1930's, and even some from the 1800's!*
- *The wrong sides of some printed fabrics resemble faded, worn versions of the right sides of the fabrics. Using the wrong side of a fabric exclusively or mixing it with the right side of the print can lend a soft look to your quilt.*

- *Several types of batting, especially those that are all-cotton, shrink when washed. A gentle washing after quilting may help slightly shrink the batting and give your quilt that wrinkled, antique look.*
- *Scrap quilts often look old even if they are brand-new. Instead of using a planned fabric scheme, substitute scraps of the same color family, just like the quilters of yesteryear did in our Zigzag Quilt and Patriotic Gem Quilt, page 72.*
- *Give your fabrics instant "age" by tea dyeing. Make a tea-dye bath using 3 to 4 regular tea bags per quart of hot tap water. Let the tea bags steep for 15 minutes before removing. Soak prewashed fabrics in the tea for 15 to 30 minutes, depending on the degree of "aging" you wish. Rinse well with cool water, squeeze, and iron dry.*
- *Commercial dyes are available to give new fabrics an antique look. Check with your local quilt shop or fabric store for these supplies.*

DOUBLE WEDDING RING COLLECTION

During the 1930's, a revival of interest in patchwork swept the country. A new generation of quilters enjoyed thousands of fresh and rediscovered patterns from magazines, newspapers, and mail-order catalogs. With such widespread appeal, several designs emerged as instant classics, including the beloved Double Wedding Ring. It has become one of the most often-pieced quilts in America, but the pretty curved pieces also make it one of the most challenging to create. We've helped simplify the pattern by using time-saving rotary cutting and strip piecing, along with traditional templates. The open areas are enhanced with charming quilted flowers.

ften presented to newlyweds, the Double Wedding Ring pattern symbolizes the devotion of marriage. You can re-create the romance of the traditional quilt in a fraction of the time with our sweet wall hanging! Pieced in soft pastels, it's made using four rings from the basic design and a simple quilting pattern.

DOUBLE WEDDING RING QUILT

SKILL LEVEL: 1 2 3 4 5
RING SIZE: 18" diameter
QUILT SIZE: 96" x 109"

YARDAGE REQUIREMENTS

Yardage is based on 45"w fabric.

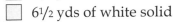 8½ yds **total** of assorted pastel prints

☐ 6½ yds of white solid

▨ 5/8 yd of peach solid

▨ 5/8 yd of green solid
8¾ yds for backing
1¼ yds for binding
120" x 120" batting

ROTARY CUTTING

All measurements include a ¼" seam allowance. Follow Rotary Cutting, page 144, to cut fabric.

1. **From pastel prints:** ▨
   - Cut a total of 26 selvage-to-selvage **narrow strips** 2½"w.
   - Cut a total of 52 selvage-to-selvage **wide strips** 4¼"w.

2. **From peach solid:** ▨
   - Cut 8 selvage-to-selvage strips 2½"w. From these strips, cut 127 **squares** 2½" x 2½".

3. **From green solid:** ▨
   - Cut 8 selvage-to-selvage strips 2½"w. From these strips, cut 127 **squares** 2½" x 2½".

ASSEMBLING THE STRIP SETS

Follow Piecing and Pressing, page 146, to make strip sets.

1. Beginning and ending with narrow strips, assemble 2 **narrow** and 4 **wide strips** in random color order to make **Strip Set**. Make 13 **Strip Sets**.

Strip Set (make 13)

TEMPLATE CUTTING

*Use patterns **AA**, **AB**, **C**, and **D**, page 27, and follow Template Cutting, page 146, to cut fabric.*

1. From 4 **Strip Sets**, use **Template AA** to cut out 254 **AA Units**, placing center line of template on seams as shown in **Fig. 1**.

Fig. 1

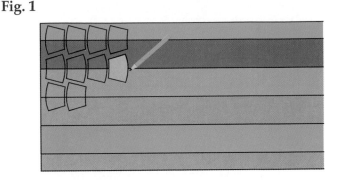

2. From remaining 9 **Strip Sets**, use **Template AB** to cut out 254 **AB Units** and 254 **Reversed AB Units**, placing center line of template on seams.

3. From white solid, cut 127 **C's** using **Template C** and 56 **D's** using **Template D**.

ASSEMBLING THE QUILT TOP

Follow Piecing and Pressing, page 146, to make quilt top.

1. Assemble 1 **Reversed AB Unit**, 1 **AA Unit**, and 1 **AB Unit** to make **Unit 1**. Make 254 **Unit 1's**.

Unit 1 (make 254)

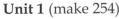

2. Assemble 2 **squares** and 1 **Unit 1** to make **Unit 2**. Make 127 **Unit 2's**.

Unit 2 (make 127)

3. (*Note: For curved seams in Steps 3 - 8, match centers and pin at center and at dots, then match and pin between these points. Sew seam with convex edge on bottom next to feed dogs.*) Assemble 1 **C** and 1 **Unit 1** to make **Unit 3**. Make 127 **Unit 3's**.

Unit 3 (make 127)

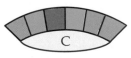

4. Assemble 1 **Unit 2** and 1 **Unit 3** to make **Unit 4**. Make 127 **Unit 4's**.

Unit 4 (make 127)

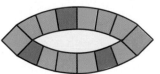

23

5. Assemble 4 **Unit 4's** and 1 **D** to make **Unit 5**. Make 28 **Unit 5's**.

Unit 5 (make 28)

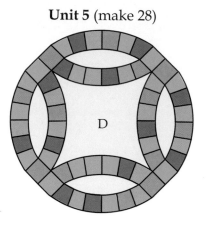

6. Assemble 2 **Unit 4's** and 1 **D** to make **Unit 6**. Make 2 **Unit 6's**.

Unit 6 (make 2)

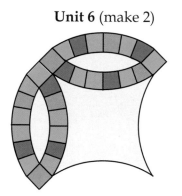

7. Assemble 1 **Unit 4** and 1 **D** to make **Unit 7**. Make 11 **Unit 7's**.

Unit 7 (make 11)

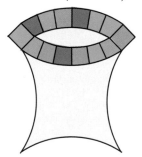

8. Follow **Assembly Diagram** to assemble **Unit 5's**, **Unit 6's**, **Unit 7's**, and remaining **D's** into horizontal **Rows**. Assemble **Rows** to complete **Quilt Top**.

COMPLETING THE QUILT

1. Follow **Quilting**, page 152, to mark, layer, and quilt, using **Quilting Diagram** as a suggestion. Our quilt is hand quilted using **Quilting Pattern A**, page 27.

2. Cut a 42" square of binding fabric. Follow **Making Continuous Bias Strip Binding**, page 155, to make approximately 14 yds of 2½"w bias binding.

3. Follow Steps 1 and 2 of **Attaching Binding with Mitered Corners**, page 156, to pin binding to front of quilt. Sew binding to quilt, easing curves and leaving a 2" overlap. Trim off excess binding and stitch overlap in place. Fold binding over to quilt backing and pin in place, covering stitching line. Blindstitch binding to backing.

Quilt Top Diagram

Quilting Diagram

DOUBLE WEDDING RING WALL HANGING

SKILL LEVEL: 1 2 3 4 5
RING SIZE: 18" diameter
WALL HANGING SIZE: 31" x 31"

YARDAGE REQUIREMENTS

Yardage is based on 45"w fabric.

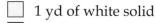 1¾ yds **total** of assorted pastel prints

☐ 1 yd of white solid

▨ ⅛ yd of peach print

▨ ⅛ yd of blue print
1¼ yds for backing
¾ yd for binding
35" x 35" batting

ROTARY CUTTING

All measurements include a ¼" seam allowance. Follow
Rotary Cutting, page 144, to cut fabric.

1. **From pastel prints:** ◪
   - Cut a total of 2 selvage-to-selvage **strips** 2½"w.
   - Cut a total of 5 selvage-to-selvage **strips** 4¼"w.

2. **From peach print:** ▨
   - Cut 1 selvage-to-selvage strip 2½"w. From this strip, cut 12 **squares** 2½" x 2½".

3. **From blue print:** ▨
   - Cut 1 selvage-to-selvage strip 2½"w. From this strip, cut 12 **squares** 2½" x 2½".

ASSEMBLING THE WALL HANGING TOP

Follow Piecing and Pressing, page 146, to make wall hanging top.

1. Beginning and ending with narrow strips, assemble **strips** in random color order to make 1 **Strip Set**.

Strip Set (make 1)

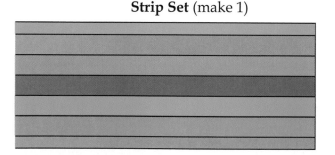

2. Refer to Steps 1 and 2 of **Template Cutting** for **Double Wedding Ring Quilt**, page 23, to cut 24 **AA Units**, 24 **AB Units**, and 24 **Reversed AB Units** from **Strip Set**. From white solid, cut 12 **C's** using **Template C** and 4 **D's** using **Template D**.

3. Follow Steps 1 - 4 of **Assembling the Quilt Top** for **Double Wedding Ring Quilt**, page 23, to make 12 **Unit 4's**.

4. Follow Steps 5 and 6 of **Assembling the Quilt Top** for **Double Wedding Ring Quilt**, page 24, to make 2 **Unit 5's** and 2 **Unit 6's**.

5. Assemble **Unit 5's** and **Unit 6's** to complete **Wall Hanging Top**.

COMPLETING THE WALL HANGING

1. Follow **Quilting**, page 152, to mark, layer, and quilt, using **Quilting Diagram** as a suggestion. Our wall hanging is hand quilted using **Quilting Pattern B**.

2. Cut a 22" square of binding fabric. Follow **Making Continuous Bias Strip Binding**, page 155, to make approximately 5 yds of 2½"w bias binding.

3. Follow Step 3 of **Completing the Quilt** for **Double Wedding Ring Quilt**, page 24, to attach binding to wall hanging.

Wall Hanging Top Diagram

Quilting Diagram

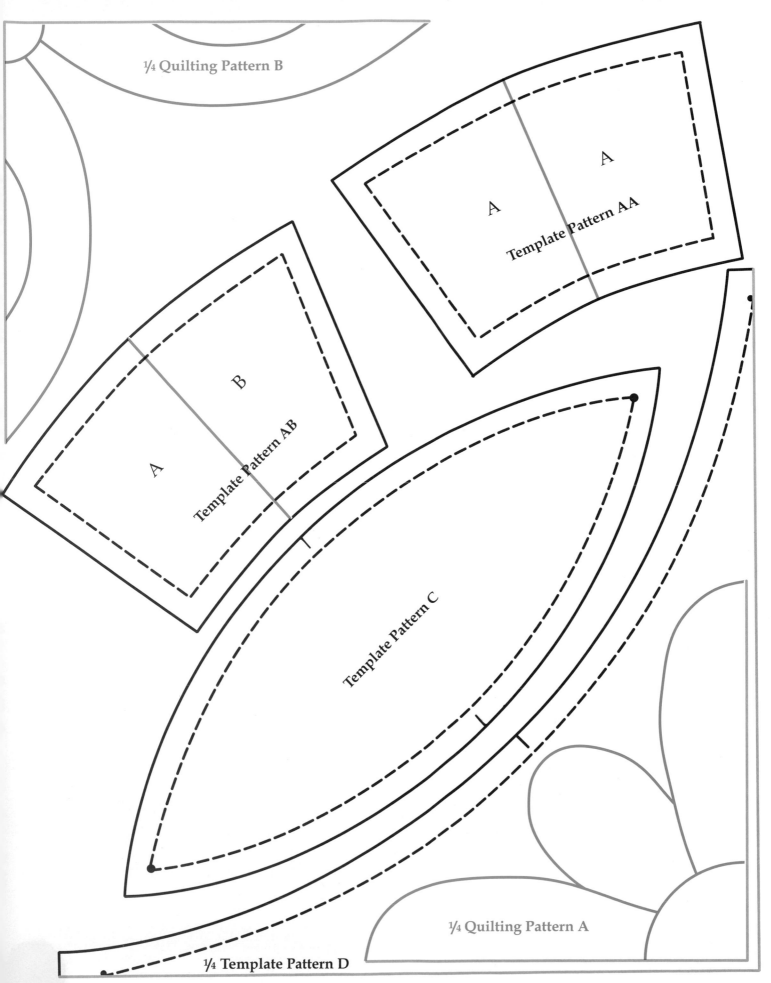

¼ Quilting Pattern B

A

A

Template Pattern AA

B

A

Template Pattern AB

Template Pattern C

¼ Quilting Pattern A

¼ Template Pattern D

PINEAPPLE QUILT

The pattern in this Log Cabin variation represents a traditional Colonial symbol of hospitality — the pineapple. This design was a favorite for frontier women, who often longed for touches of the refined lifestyle they had enjoyed before moving westward. Log Cabin quilts are known for their simplicity, and to make our version even easier we eliminated a step. Instead of stitching on a foundation block, we simply pieced the fabric strips around a center square and rotary cut them into shape! The striped border for our Pineapple quilt is a breeze to add.

PINEAPPLE QUILT

SKILL LEVEL: 1 2 **3** 4 5
BLOCK SIZE: 15" x 15"
QUILT SIZE: 91" x 106"

YARDAGE REQUIREMENTS

Yardage is based on 45"w fabric.

■ 10 yds **total** of assorted dark prints

◪ 6 yds **total** of assorted light prints
8¼ yds for backing
1 yd for binding
120" x 120" batting

You will also need:
12½" x 12½" square rotary cutting ruler

CUTTING OUT THE PIECES

All measurements include a ¼" seam allowance. Follow
Rotary Cutting, *page 144, to cut fabric.*

1. **From assorted dark prints:** ■
    *   Cut a total of 142 selvage-to-selvage **strips** 2"w.
    *   From remaining fabric, cut a total of 30 **center squares** 3½" x 3½".
2. **From assorted light prints:** ◪
    *   Cut a total of 97 selvage-to-selvage **strips** 2"w.

ASSEMBLING THE QUILT TOP

Follow ***Piecing and Pressing***, *page 146, to make quilt top. Assemble blocks in alternating* ***light*** *and* ***dark*** *rounds, adding strips in random fashion within each round. Use square rotary cutting ruler to align, measure, and cut strips throughout block construction.*

1. For ruler placement guidelines, refer to **Fig. 1** and use a removable marker to precisely mark each **center square** in half horizontally, vertically, and diagonally on the right side of fabric.

    Fig. 1

2. (*Note:* For Steps 2 - 7, refer to **Block Diagram**, page 32, and **Table**, page 32, to make block. The **Block Diagram** shows ruler placement guidelines in pink and blue. Use the pink guidelines when adding light rounds and blue guidelines when adding dark rounds. Use the **Table** measurements to align ruler with placement guidelines.) Referring to **Fig. 2**, assemble 1 **center square** and 4 light **strips**, trimming off remainder of each strip after stitching; open and press. Referring to **Fig. 3**, align **L1** measurement on ruler with pink

placement lines on **center square**. Trim off fabric extending beyond ruler edges. Referring to **Fig. 4**, rotate square ½ turn and repeat for opposite side of square to make **Unit 1**.

Fig. 2

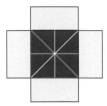

Fig. 3

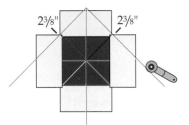

Fig. 4

Unit 1

3. Referring to **Fig. 5**, assemble **Unit 1** and 4 dark **strips**, trimming off remainder of each strip after stitching; open and press. Referring to **Fig. 6**, align **D2** measurements on ruler with blue placement lines on **Unit 1**. Cut along ruler edges. Referring to **Fig. 7**, rotate square ½ turn and repeat for opposite side of square to make **Unit 2**.

Fig. 5

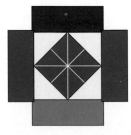

Fig. 6

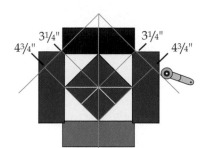

Fig. 7

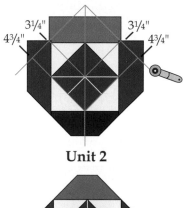

Unit 2

4. Referring to **Fig. 8**, assemble **Unit 2** and 4 light **strips**, trimming off remainder of each strip after stitching; open and press. Referring to **Fig. 9**, align **L3** measurements on ruler with pink placement lines on **Unit 2**. Trim off fabric extending beyond ruler edges. Referring to **Fig. 10**, rotate square ¹/₂ turn and repeat for opposite side of square to make **Unit 3**.

Fig. 8

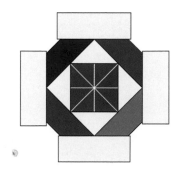

Fig. 9

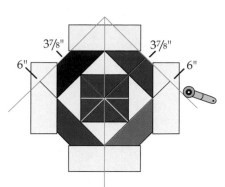

Fig. 10

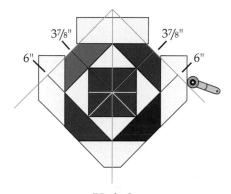
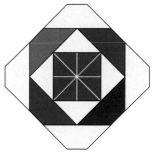

Unit 3

5. Repeat Steps 3 and 4 to add rounds **D4**, **L5**, **D6**, **L7**, and **D8** to make **Unit 4**.

Unit 4

6. Add dark **strips** to **Unit 4**. Align **D9** measurements on ruler with blue placement lines on square. Cut 1 corner at a time until all 4 corners are trimmed to make **Unit 5**.

Unit 5

7. Repeat Step 6 to add round **D10** to complete **Block**.

Block

8. Repeat Steps 2 - 7 to make 30 **Blocks**.
9. Referring to **Quilt Top Diagram**, assemble 5 **Blocks** to make **Row**. Make 6 **Rows**. Assemble **Rows** to complete center section of quilt top.
10. Assemble 20 **strips**, alternating light and dark, to make a **Strip Set** 30½"l. Make 3 **Strip Sets**. Cut across **Strip Sets** at 8" intervals to make a total of 14 **Unit 6's**.

Strip Set (make 3) **Unit 6** (make 14)

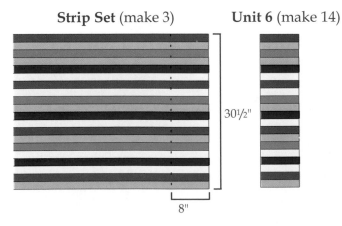

30½"

8"

11. Sew short edges of all **Unit 6's** together to make 1 pieced strip. From this strip, cut 2 **Top/Bottom Border Units** 94"l and 2 **Side Border Units** 109"l.
12. Referring to **Quilt Top Diagram**, follow **Adding Mitered Borders**, page 151, to attach **Top**, **Bottom**, then **Side Border Units** to complete **Quilt Top**.

COMPLETING THE QUILT

1. Follow **Quilting**, page 152, to mark, layer, and quilt, using **Quilting Diagram** as a suggestion. Our quilt is hand quilted.
2. Cut a 33" square of binding fabric. Follow **Binding**, page 155, to bind quilt using 2½"w bias binding with mitered corners.

Block Diagram

Table

Round	Light Guideline Measurements (shown in pink)		Dark Guideline Measurements (shown in blue)	
	INSIDE	OUTSIDE	INSIDE	OUTSIDE
L1	2³/₈"	—		
D2			3¹/₄"	4³/₄"
L3	3⁷/₈"	6"		
D4			4³/₄"	6¹/₄"
L5	5³/₈"	7¹/₂"		
D6			6¹/₄"	7³/₄"
L7	6⁷/₈"	9"		
D8			7³/₄"	9¹/₄"
D9			7³/₄"	9¹/₄"
D10			7³/₄"	9¹/₄"

32

Quilt Top Diagram

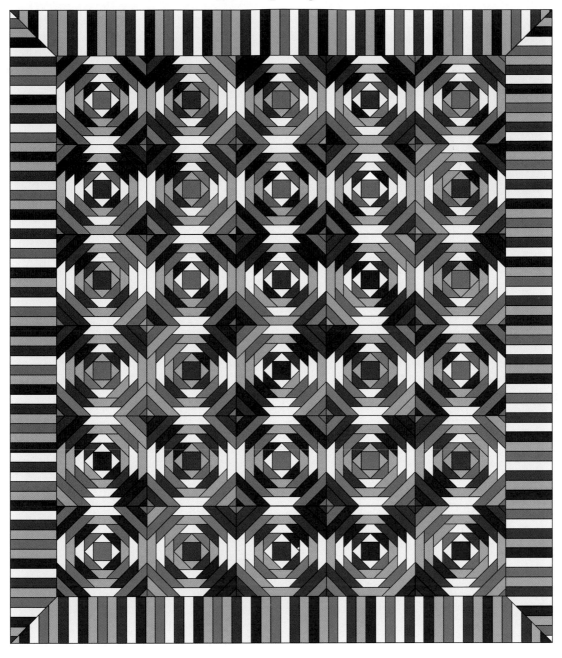

Quilting Diagram

TRIP AROUND THE WORLD COLLECTION

The kaleidoscope look of the Trip Around the World pattern was especially appealing to quilters of the 1930's. They loved its cheery effect, but they also appreciated its efficiency — they could create a stunning quilt using scraps of worn clothing or other fabrics. Although the design was frequently pieced only in solid fabrics, a variety of prints and solids was used to create our impressive quilt. For our version, we saved time and effort by assembling the diagonal units using rotary-cut, strip-pieced sets. We accented the concentric rows with simple grid quilting and a blanket-stitched edging along the outer row. Our blanket stitching was done by hand, but many machines today can do this decorative stitching for you. Either way, it's a nice touch!

*W*e chose soft pastels for our lap quilt, a faster — and even easier — version of the Trip Around the World pattern. It's made using the same simple methods, but its smaller size will give you colorful results in a snap!

TRIP AROUND THE WORLD QUILT

SKILL LEVEL: 1 2 3 4 5
QUILT SIZE: 78" x 93"

YARDAGE REQUIREMENTS

Yardage is based on 45"w fabric.

- 4 yds of white solid
- 1⁵/₈ yds of pink solid
- ⁵/₈ yd **each** of light blue print, light blue solid, light yellow print, light yellow solid, purple print, purple solid, and light green print
- ³/₈ yd **each** of light green solid, orange print, orange solid, blue print, blue solid, pink print, green print, green solid, yellow print, and yellow solid
- ¹/₈ yd **each** of dark purple print and dark purple solid
- 5⁵/₈ yds for backing
- 1 yd for binding
- 90" x 108" batting

You will also need:
pink embroidery floss

CUTTING OUT THE PIECES

All measurements include a ¼" seam allowance. Follow Rotary Cutting, page 144, to cut fabric.

1. **From white solid:**
   - Cut 56 selvage-to-selvage **strips** 2¹/₄"w.

2. **From pink solid:**
   - Cut 20 selvage-to-selvage **strips** 2¹/₄"w. From 1 strip, cut 4 **squares** 2¹/₄" x 2¹/₄".

3. **From light blue print, light blue solid, light yellow print, light yellow solid, purple print, and purple solid:**
   - Cut 8 selvage-to-selvage **strips** 2¹/₄"w from *each* fabric.

4. **From light green print:**
   - Cut 6 selvage-to-selvage **strips** 2¹/₄"w. From 1 strip, cut 4 **squares** 2¹/₄" x 2¹/₄".

5. **From light green solid, orange print, orange solid, blue print, and blue solid:**
   - Cut 5 selvage-to-selvage **strips** 2¹/₄"w from *each* fabric.

6. **From pink print:**
   - Cut 4 selvage-to-selvage **strips** 2¹/₄"w. From 1 strip, cut 4 **squares** 2¹/₄" x 2¹/₄".

7. **From green print, green solid, yellow print, and yellow solid:**
   - Cut 3 selvage-to-selvage **strips** 2¹/₄"w from *each* fabric.

8. **From dark purple print:**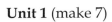
   - Cut 1 selvage-to-selvage strip 2¹/₄"w. From this strip, cut 2 **squares** 2¹/₄" x 2¹/₄". Cut remainder of strip in half to make 2 **strips** 2¹/₄" x 18".

9. **From dark purple solid:**
   - Cut 1 **strip** 2¹/₄" x 18".

ASSEMBLING THE QUILT TOP

*Follow **Piecing and Pressing**, page 146, to make quilt top.*

1. Assemble 2¹/₄" x 18" **strips** to make 1 **Strip Set A**. Cut across **Strip Set A** at 2¹/₄" intervals to make 7 **Unit 1's**.

Strip Set A (make 1)   **Unit 1** (make 7)

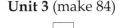

2. Assemble **strips** to make **Strip Set B**. Make 3 **Strip Set B's**. Cut across **Strip Set B's** at 2¹/₄" intervals to make 48 **Unit 2's**.

Strip Set B (make 3)   **Unit 2** (make 48)

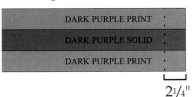

3. Assemble **strips** to make **Strip Set C**. Make 5 **Strip Set C's**. Cut across **Strip Set C's** at 2¹/₄" intervals to make 84 **Unit 3's**.

Strip Set C (make 5)   **Unit 3** (make 84)

4. Assemble **strips** to make **Strip Set D**. Make 8 **Strip Set D's**. Cut across **Strip Set D** at 2¼" intervals to make 132 **Unit 4's**.

Strip Set D (make 8)　　**Unit 4 (make 132)**

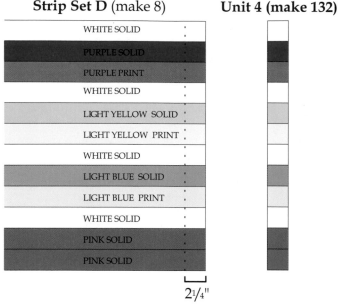

2¼"

5. To assemble quilt top, refer to **Assembly Diagram** and follow Steps 5 - 8. Quilt top will be assembled in diagonal rows running from upper right to lower left. Symbols placed in the squares of the **Diagram** will help you determine where one Unit ends and another begins. For correct color sequence to develop, some Partial Units will be used. To make a Partial Unit, use a seam ripper to remove unneeded squares from a Unit.

6. Begin assembly by choosing any one of the longer diagonal rows in the **Diagram**. Arrange **Units**, **Partial Units**, and **squares** as indicated to make up row. Sew pieces together along short edges to complete row. Carefully check sewn row to make sure that the correct number of squares are present and colors are in the correct order. All other rows will be based on this first row.

7. Referring to **Diagram**, choose the diagonal row directly above your first sewn row. Repeat Step 6 to sew pieces together to make row. Sew the two completed rows together.

8. Moving up one row at a time, continue to arrange and sew pieces into rows, then sew rows together until top left half of quilt top is complete. Repeat to complete lower right half of quilt top.

9. To trim outer edges of quilt top, align ¼" marking on ruler (shown in yellow) with outer seam intersections as shown in **Fig. 1** and trim off excess. Machine stitch ⅛" from cut edge to prevent bias edge from stretching.

Fig. 1

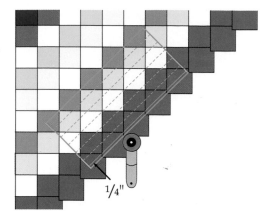

¼"

10. Referring to photo, use 3 strands of floss to work **Blanket Stitch**, page 158, around outer edges of outer row of white squares.

COMPLETING THE QUILT

1. Follow **Quilting**, page 152, to mark, layer, and quilt. Our quilt is hand quilted in a diagonal grid (see photo).

2. Cut a 32" square of binding fabric. Follow **Binding**, page 155, to bind quilt using 2½"w bias binding with mitered corners.

Quilt Top Diagram

KEY

- ◤ Unit 1
- ⊞ Unit 2
- ⑤ Partial Unit 2
- ▢ Unit 3
- ✳ Partial Unit 3
- ▽ Unit 4
- ☆ Partial Unit 4
- ◎ Square
- ＼ Designates Where 2 Partial Units Meet

TRIP AROUND THE WORLD LAP QUILT

SKILL LEVEL: 1 2 3 4 5
LAP QUILT SIZE: 52" x 67"

YARDAGE REQUIREMENTS

Yardage is based on 45"w fabric.

- ☐ 1³/₈ yds of white print
- ■ 1³/₈ yds of pink print
- ☐ ⁵/₈ yd of large blue print
- ■ ¹/₂ yd of small blue print
- ■ ¹/₂ yd of large purple print
- ■ ³/₈ yd of small green print
- ☐ ³/₈ yd of large green print
- ■ ¹/₈ yd of small purple print

3⁵/₈ yds for backing
³/₄ yd for binding
72" x 90" batting

You will also need:
pink embroidery floss

CUTTING OUT THE PIECES

All measurements include a ¹/₄" seam allowance. Follow
Rotary Cutting, *page 144, to cut fabric.*

1. **From white print:** ☐
    - Cut 13 selvage-to-selvage **strips** 3¹/₄"w. From 1 strip, cut 8 **squares** 3¹/₄" x 3¹/₄".

2. **From pink print:** ■
    - Cut 13 selvage-to-selvage **strips** 3¹/₄"w. From 1 strip, cut 12 **squares** 3¹/₄" x 3¹/₄".

3. **From large blue print:** ☐
    - Cut 5 selvage-to-selvage **strips** 3¹/₄"w. From 1 strip, cut 4 **squares** 3¹/₄" x 3¹/₄".

4. **From small blue print:** ■
    - Cut 4 selvage-to-selvage **strips** 3¹/₄"w.

5. **From large purple print:** ■
    - Cut 4 selvage-to-selvage **strips** 3¹/₄"w. From 1 strip, cut 4 **squares** 3¹/₄" x 3¹/₄".

6. **From small green print:** ■
    - Cut 3 selvage-to-selvage **strips** 3¹/₄"w.

7. **From large green print:** ☐
    - Cut 3 selvage-to-selvage **strips** 3¹/₄"w.

8. **From small purple print:** ■
    - Cut 5 **squares** 3¹/₄" x 3¹/₄".

ASSEMBLING THE QUILT TOP

Follow **Piecing and Pressing**, *page 146, to make quilt top.*

1. Assemble **strips** to make 1 **Strip Set A**. Cut across **Strip Set A** at 3¹/₄" intervals to make 12 **Unit 1's**.

Strip Set A (make 1)　　　　**Unit 1** (make 12)

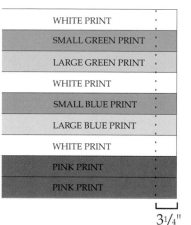

2. Assemble **strips** to make 1 **Strip Set B**. Cut across **Strip Set B** at 3¹/₄" intervals to make 8 **Unit 2's**.

Strip Set B (make 1)　　　　**Unit 2** (make 8)

3. Assemble **strips** to make **Strip Set C**. Make 3 **Strip Set C's**. Cut across **Strip Set C's** at 3¹/₄" intervals to make 36 **Unit 3's**.

Strip Set C (make 3)　　　　**Unit 3** (make 36)

4. Assemble **strips** to make 1 **Strip Set D**. Cut across **Strip Set D** at 3¹/₄" intervals to make 8 **Unit 4's**.

Strip Set D (make 1)　　　　**Unit 4** (make 8)

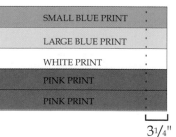
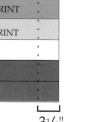

5. Assemble **strips** to make 1 **Strip Set E**. Cut across **Strip Set E** at 3¼" intervals to make 8 **Unit 5's**.

Strip Set E (make 1)   **Unit 5** (make 8)

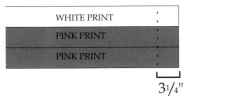

3¼"

6. Referring to **Assembly Diagram** on this page, follow Steps 5 - 10 of **Assembling the Quilt Top** for **Trip Around the World Quilt**, page 38, to assemble pieces, trim edges, and add embroidery to complete **Quilt Top**.

COMPLETING THE QUILT

1. Follow **Quilting**, page 152, to mark, layer, and quilt. Our quilt is hand quilted in a grid pattern (see photo).
2. Cut a 27" square of binding fabric. Follow **Binding**, page 155, to bind quilt using 2½"w bias binding with mitered corners.

Quilt Top Diagram

Assembly Diagram

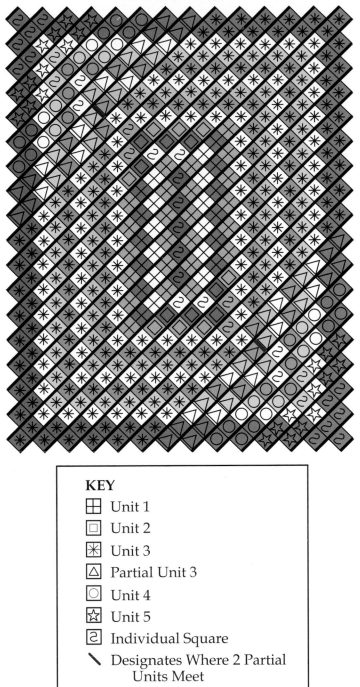

KEY	
⊞	Unit 1
▢	Unit 2
✳	Unit 3
△	Partial Unit 3
◯	Unit 4
☆	Unit 5
�	Individual Square
╲	Designates Where 2 Partial Units Meet

SPRING BOUQUET COLLECTION

The real beauty of this feminine quilt is the simplicity of its design. The large center squares within the pattern provide a showcase for pretty print fabrics. We chose a variety of enchanting florals that are reminiscent of a lush English garden. To complete each block, we rotary cut triangles from strip-pieced sets using a special ruler that allows you to produce accurate angles with ease. And with no sashing pieces needed, the quilt is especially quick to assemble. Our rounded quilting pattern gives the blocks a circular illusion — without the difficulty of piecing curved shapes!

44

Add a feminine flourish to your decor with these spring-fresh accessories. Our floral table topper is a miniature version of the breezy quilt — and it's just as easy! Drape it over an accent table and coordinating table skirt for a charming touch. To create our topiary wall hanging (opposite), we employed a popular technique in contemporary quilting called colorwash — a method of arranging the color values of different prints to create a dramatic overall effect. Elegant bow and cable quilting add subtle texture.

A trio of coordinating throw pillows will be just the right touch for your bed. Springtime beauty is sealed into our feminine envelope pillow, which is accented with ribbons and flowers. Our Spring Bouquet quilt block becomes a comfy pillow when finished with soft binding. Enhanced with wired-ribbon bows, the romantic roll pillow is wrapped in a pieced band of floral prints.

SPRING BOUQUET QUILT

SKILL LEVEL: 1 2 3 4 5
BLOCK SIZE: 12" x 12"
QUILT SIZE: 85" x 97"

YARDAGE REQUIREMENTS

Yardage is based on 45"w fabric.

- 5$\frac{1}{8}$ yds of large floral print
- 3$\frac{5}{8}$ yds of small floral print
- 1$\frac{3}{4}$ yds of white print
- 1$\frac{3}{4}$ yds of green print
  7$\frac{3}{4}$ yds for backing
  1 yd for binding
  120" x 120" batting

You will also need:
  Companion Angle™ Rotary Cutting Ruler (made by EZ International)

CUTTING OUT THE PIECES

All measurements include a ¼" seam allowance. Follow **Rotary Cutting**, *page 144, to cut fabric.*

1. **From large floral print:**
   - Cut 8 selvage-to-selvage strips 9"w. From these strips, cut 32 **squares** 9" x 9".
   - Cut 2 lengthwise strips 6½" x 100" for **side borders**.
   - Cut 2 lengthwise strips 6½" x 76" for **top/bottom borders**.
   - From remaining fabric, cut 10 additional **squares** 9" x 9".

2. **From small floral print:**
   - Cut 42 selvage-to-selvage **strips** 2¾"w.

3. **From white print:**
   - Cut 21 selvage-to-selvage **strips** 2½"w.

4. **From green print:**
   - Cut 21 selvage-to-selvage **strips** 2½"w.

ASSEMBLING THE QUILT TOP

Follow **Piecing and Pressing**, *page 146, to make quilt top.*

1. Assemble **strips** to make 21 **Strip Set A's** and 21 **Strip Set B's**.

Strip Set A (make 21)   **Strip Set B** (make 21)

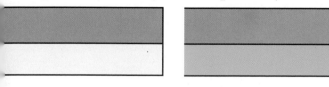

2. Line up 9" sewing line (dashed line) on Companion Angle™ ruler (4¾" from top of ruler) with bottom edge of **Strip Set A** (**Fig. 1**). Cut on both sides of ruler to make **Unit 1**. Make 84 **Unit 1's**. Repeat with **Strip Set B's** to make 84 **Unit 2's**.

Fig. 1

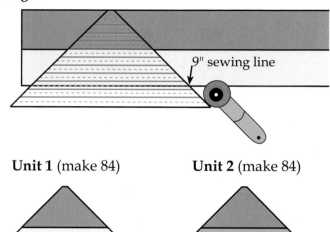

Unit 1 (make 84)   Unit 2 (make 84)

3. Assemble 4 **Unit 1's** and 1 **square** to make **Block A**. Make 21 **Block A's**. Assemble 4 **Unit 2's** and 1 **square** to make **Block B**. Make 21 **Block B's**.

Block A (make 21)   **Block B** (make 21)

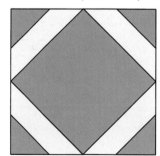 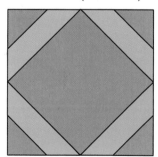

4. Assemble 3 **Block A's** and 3 **Block B's** to make **Row**. Make 7 **Rows**.

Row (make 7)

5. Referring to **Quilt Top Diagram**, page 48, assemble **Rows** to make center section of quilt top.

6. Follow **Adding Squared Borders**, page 151, to attach **top**, **bottom**, then **side borders** to center section to complete **Quilt Top**.

COMPLETING THE QUILT

1. Follow **Quilting**, page 152, to mark, layer, and quilt, using **Quilting Diagram** as a suggestion. Our quilt is hand quilted using **Quilting Pattern**, page 52.
2. Cut a 32" square of binding fabric. Follow **Binding**, page 155, to bind quilt using 2½"w bias binding with mitered corners.

Quilt Top Diagram

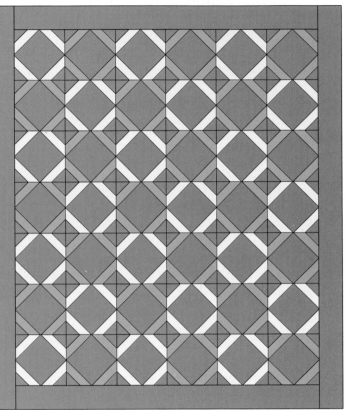

Quilting Diagram

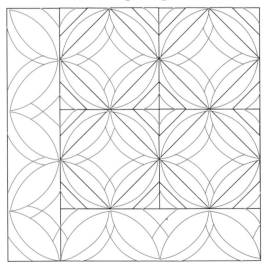

BOUQUET BLOCK PILLOW

PILLOW SIZE: 12½" x 12½"

SUPPLIES
Yardage is based on 45"w fabric.

⅛ yd of small floral print
⅛ yd of green print
9" x 9" square of large floral print
16" x 16" pillow top backing
12½" x 12½" pillow back
¼ yd for binding
16" x 16" batting
polyester fiberfill
Companion Angle™ Rotary Cutting Ruler (made by EZ International)

MAKING THE PILLOW
*All measurements include a ¼" seam allowance. Follow **Rotary Cutting**, page 144, to cut fabric. Follow **Piecing and Pressing**, page 146, to make pillow.*

1. Cut 1 selvage-to-selvage strip 2½"w from green print and 1 selvage-to-selvage strip 2¾"w from small floral print.
2. Using strips and 9" x 9" square, refer to Steps 1 - 3 of **Assembling the Quilt Top** for **Spring Bouquet Quilt**, page 47, to make 1 **Block B**.
3. Follow Step 1 of **Completing the Quilt** for **Spring Bouquet Quilt**, this page, to quilt pillow top; trim backing and batting even with pillow top edges.
4. Place pillow back and pillow top wrong sides together. Sew pieces together, leaving an opening for stuffing.
5. Stuff pillow with fiberfill and sew opening closed.
6. From binding fabric, cut a 2" x 54" strip, pieced as necessary. Press strip in half lengthwise with wrong sides together. Follow **Attaching Binding with Mitered Corners**, page 156, to bind pillow.

BEDSIDE TABLE TOPPER

BLOCK SIZE: 12" x 12"
TABLE TOPPER SIZE: 50" x 50"

YARDAGE REQUIREMENTS
Yardage is based on 45"w fabric.

1⅞ yds of large floral print
⅞ yd of small floral print
½ yd of green print
⅜ yd of white print
3¼ yds for backing
⅞ yd for binding
72" x 90" batting

You will also need:
Companion Angle™ Rotary Cutting Ruler (made by EZ International)

CUTTING OUT THE PIECES

All measurements include a ¼" seam allowance. Follow Rotary Cutting, page 144, to cut fabric.

1. **From large floral print:**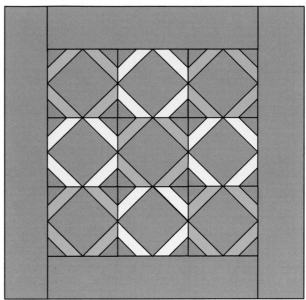
   - Cut 1 selvage-to-selvage strip 9"w. From this strip, cut 4 **squares** 9" x 9".
   - Cut 2 lengthwise strips 7½" x 50½" for **long borders**.
   - Cut 2 lengthwise strips 7½" x 36½" for **short borders**.
   - From remaining fabric, cut 5 additional **squares** 9" x 9".

2. **From small floral print:**
   - Cut 9 selvage-to-selvage **strips** 2¾"w.

3. **From green print:**
   - Cut 5 selvage-to-selvage **strips** 2½"w.

4. **From white print:**
   - Cut 4 selvage-to-selvage **strips** 2½"w.

ASSEMBLING THE TABLE TOPPER
Follow Piecing and Pressing, page 146, to make table topper.

1. Assemble **strips** to make 4 **Strip Set A's** and 5 **Strip Set B's.**

Strip Set A (make 4)   **Strip Set B (make 5)**

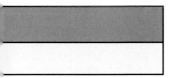   

2. Follow Steps 2 and 3 of **Assembling the Quilt Top** for **Spring Bouquet Quilt**, page 47, to make 4 **Block A's** and 5 **Block B's**. (You will need 16 **Unit 1's** and 20 **Unit 2's** to make Blocks.)
3. Referring to **Table Topper Diagram**, assemble **Block A's** and **Block B's** to make center section of table topper.
4. Attach **short**, then **long borders** to center section to complete **Table Topper**.

COMPLETING THE TABLE TOPPER
1. Follow **Quilting**, page 152, to mark, layer, and quilt, using **Quilting Diagram**, page 48, as a suggestion. Our table topper is hand quilted using **Quilting Pattern**, page 52.
2. Cut a 26" square of binding fabric. Follow **Binding**, page 155, to bind table topper using 2½"w bias binding with mitered corners.

Table Topper Diagram

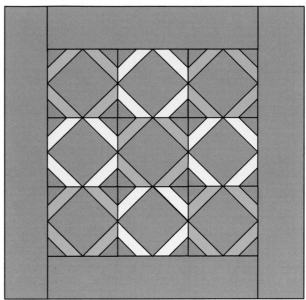

BANDED ROLL PILLOW

PILLOW SIZE: 6" x 30"

SUPPLIES
⅝ yd of green print for pillow
scraps of assorted floral prints for pieced band
¼ yd for pieced band backing
¼ yd for binding
1¾ yds of 2½"w wire-edge ribbon
2 strong rubber bands
polyester fiberfill

MAKING THE PILLOW
All measurements include a ¼" seam allowance. Follow Rotary Cutting, page 144, to cut fabric. Follow Piecing and Pressing, page 146, to make pillow.

1. From floral print scraps, cut a total of 30 squares 2½" x 2½". Assemble squares to make pieced band.

pieced band

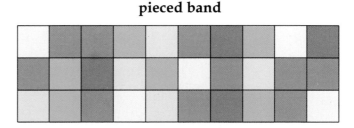

2. Cut pieced band backing 6½" x 20½". Place pieced band and pieced band backing wrong sides together and baste along long edges.
3. From binding fabric, cut 2 strips 2" x 24"; press strips in half lengthwise with wrong sides together.

4. Matching raw edges, sew 1 binding strip to front of pieced band along each long edge. Fold binding over to band backing and blindstitch in place. Trim ends of binding even with short ends of pieced band.

5. Sew short ends of pieced band together and turn right side out to complete pieced band.

6. For pillow, cut green print fabric 20" x 40". Press each short edge 1/4" to wrong side; press 5" to wrong side again and stitch in place. Sew long edges together to form a tube. Turn right side out and press.

7. Wrap 1 rubber band around tube 5" from 1 end. Stuff tube with fiberfill and wrap remaining rubber band around tube 5" from remaining end.

8. Slip pieced band over pillow, centering band and matching seams; tack in place.

9. Cut ribbon in half. Tie 1 ribbon length into a bow around each end of pillow, covering rubber bands; trim ribbon ends.

FLORAL ENVELOPE PILLOW

PILLOW SIZE: 12 1/2" x 18 1/2"

SUPPLIES
3/4 yd of large floral print for pillow front
3/4 yd of small floral print for pillow back and flap
polyester fiberfill
nosegay of artificial flowers trimmed with
    desired ribbons

MAKING THE PILLOW
All measurements include a 1/4" seam allowance. Follow Rotary Cutting, page 144, to cut fabric. Follow Piecing and Pressing, page 146, to make pillow.

1. From large floral print, cut 1 pillow front 13 3/4" x 19". For binding, cut 1 strip 2 1/2" x 36" from remaining fabric; press strip in half lengthwise with wrong sides together.

2. From small floral print, cut 1 pillow back 19" x 21". For flap on pillow back fabric piece, refer to **Fig. 1** and cut a point at 1 short edge (top).

Fig. 1

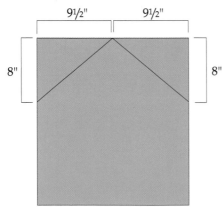

3. To bind flap on pillow back, follow **Attaching Binding with Mitered Corners**, page 156, mitering binding at point. Trim binding ends even with pillow back side edges.

4. Press 1 long edge (top) of pillow front 1/4" to wrong side and stitch in place.

5. Matching side and bottom edges, place pillow front and pillow back right sides together and stitch side and bottom edges. Clip corners, turn right side out, and press.

6. Stuff pillow lightly with fiberfill. Blindstitch point of flap in place and add nosegay to complete pillow.

TOPIARY WALL HANGING

SKILL LEVEL: 1 2 **3** 4 5
WALL HANGING SIZE: 20" x 31"

YARDAGE REQUIREMENTS
Yardage is based on 45"w fabric.

- 1/2 yd of green print
- 3/8 yd of dark green print
- 1/8 yd of floral print for inner borders
- assorted floral print scraps for topiary, leaves, and stem
- light, medium, and dark tan print fabric scraps for basket
7/8 yd for backing and hanging sleeve
3/8 yd for binding
24" x 35" batting

You will also need:
paper-backed fusible web
fabric glue

CUTTING OUT THE PIECES
All measurements include a 1/4" seam allowance. Follow Rotary Cutting, page 144, to cut fabric unless otherwise indicated.

1. **From green print:**
   - Cut 1 **background** 13 1/2" x 24 1/2".

2. **From dark green print:**
   - Cut 3 selvage-to-selvage strips 3"w. From these strips, cut 2 **top/bottom outer borders** 3" x 15" and 2 **side outer borders** 3" x 31".

3. **From floral print for inner borders:**
   - Cut 2 selvage-to-selvage strips 1 1/4"w. From these strips, cut 2 **top/bottom inner borders** 1 1/4" x 15" and 2 **side inner borders** 1 1/4" x 24 1/2".

4. **From assorted floral print scraps and tan print scraps:**
   - For topiary, cut a total of 25 floral print **squares** 2 1/2" x 2 1/2".
   - For leaves, fuse web to wrong side(s) of desired floral print(s) and cut desired **leaf shapes** from fabric(s).

- For stem, fuse web to wrong side of 1 floral print and cut **stem** 3/4" x 7 1/4".
- For basket, use patterns, page 52, and follow **Preparing Appliqué Pieces**, page 149, to cut 1 **basket center** from light tan, 2 **inner basket** pieces (1 in reverse) from medium tan, and 2 **outer basket** pieces (1 in reverse) from dark tan.

ASSEMBLING THE WALL HANGING TOP

*Follow **Piecing and Pressing**, page 146, to make wall hanging top.*

1. Assemble **squares** to make **Unit 1**. Use a compass or plate to mark a 9 1/2" diameter circle in center of **Unit 1**. Cut out circle to make **Topiary Unit**.

Unit 1

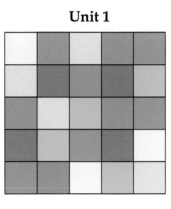

Topiary Unit

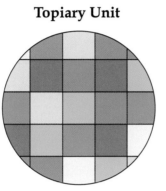

2. Using fabric glue to secure edges of **Topiary Unit**, follow **Almost Invisible Appliqué**, page 149, to stitch all pieces to **background**.
3. Attach **side**, then **top** and **bottom inner borders** to **background**.
4. Attach **top**, **bottom**, then **side outer borders** to complete **Wall Hanging Top**.

COMPLETING THE WALL HANGING

1. Follow **Quilting**, page 152, to mark, layer, and quilt, using **Quilting Diagram** as a suggestion. Our wall hanging is hand quilted using **Border Pattern**, page 52, and **Bow** and **Streamer Patterns**, page 53.
2. Follow **Making a Hanging Sleeve**, page 157, to attach hanging sleeve.
3. Follow **Binding**, page 155, to bind wall hanging using 2 1/2"w straight-grain binding with overlapped corners.

Wall Hanging Top Diagram

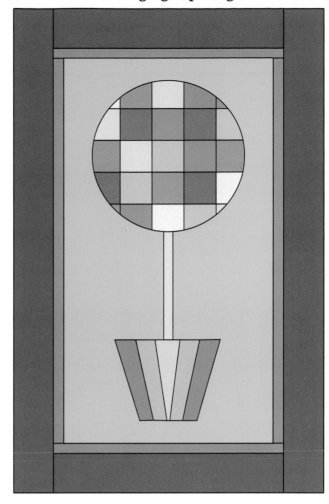

Quilting Diagram

51

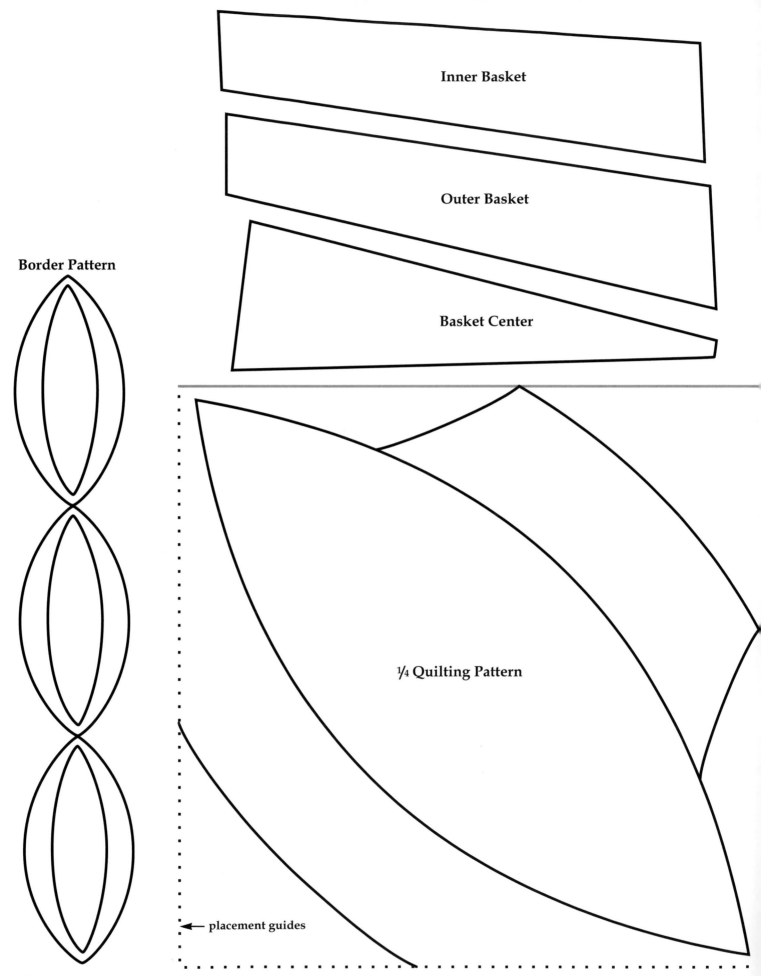

Inner Basket

Outer Basket

Basket Center

Border Pattern

¼ Quilting Pattern

← placement guides

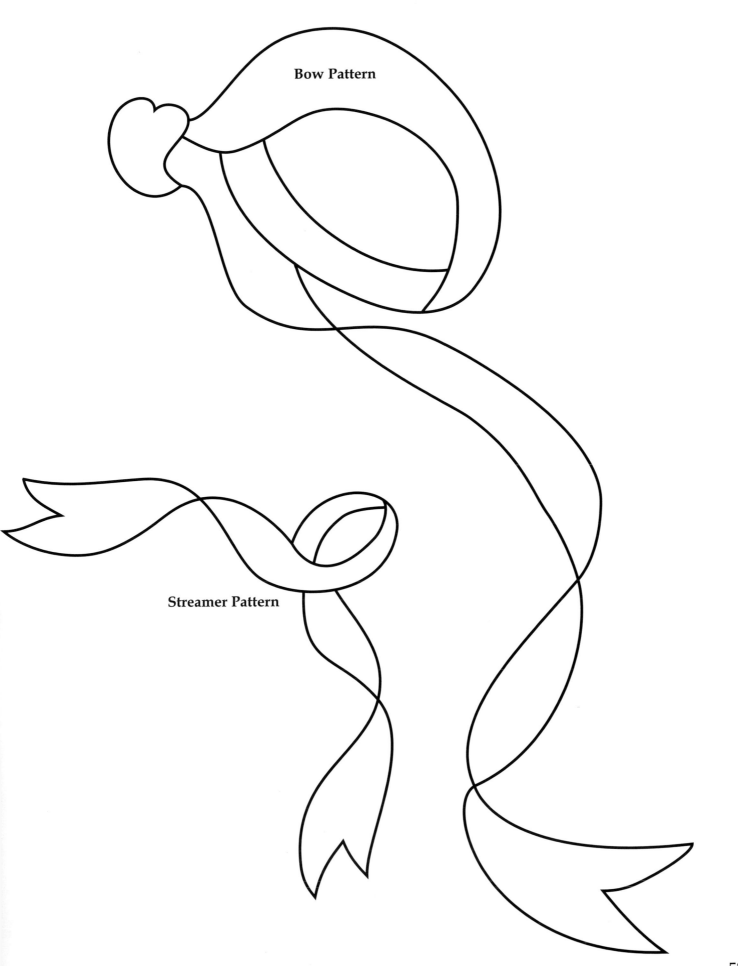

Bow Pattern

Streamer Pattern

53

OHIO ROSE

One blossom has reigned through the years as a favorite subject for appliquéd quilts: the elegant rose. Arranged in wreaths, crosses, baskets, or clusters, the patterns were given such lyrical names as Rose of Sharon, Whig Rose, and Kentucky Rose. For our Ohio Rose quilt, we created the blooms using water-soluble stabilizer — a simple method that allows the quilter to make accurate points on the petals and leaves. Machine-appliquéd onto large blocks that are joined in rows, the blossoms are surrounded by a deep, easy-to-add border that's an open canvas for elaborate feather quilting. The rose motif is repeated on the pillow flip and embellished with chain stitch embroidery.

OHIO ROSE QUILT

SKILL LEVEL: 1 2 3 4 5
BLOCK SIZE: 20" x 20"
QUILT SIZE: 94" x 109"

YARDAGE REQUIREMENTS

Yardage is based on 45"w fabric.

- 8³/₈ yds of white print
- 3¹/₄ yds of floral with blue background
- 1¹/₈ yds of green print
- ⁵/₈ yd of pink print
- ³/₈ yd of blue print
- ¹/₈ yd of pink solid
  8⁵/₈ yds for backing
  1 yd for binding
  120" x 120" batting

You will also need:
transparent monofilament thread for appliqué
5¹/₂ yds of 19"w water-soluble stabilizer
pink embroidery floss
permanent fabric marker

CUTTING OUT THE PIECES

All measurements include a ¹/₄" seam allowance. Follow
***Rotary Cutting**, page 144, to cut fabric unless otherwise
indicated.*

1. **From white print:**
    - Cut 5 selvage-to-selvage strips 21"w. From these strips, cut 9 **background squares** 21" x 21".
    - Cut 2 lengthwise strips 13" x 112" for **side outer borders**.
    - Cut 1 lengthwise strip 13" x 72" for **bottom outer border**.
    - Cut 1 lengthwise strip 27³/₄" x 72" for **pillow flip**.

2. **From floral with blue background:**
    - Cut 6 selvage-to-selvage strips 5¹/₂"w. From these strips, cut 40 **rectangle D's** 5¹/₂" x 6".
    - Cut 2 lengthwise strips 4¹/₂" x 73" for **top/bottom inner borders**.
    - Cut 2 lengthwise strips 4¹/₂" x 65" for **side inner borders**.
    - Use pattern **F**, page 61, and follow **Template Cutting**, page 146, to cut 16 **F's**.

3. **From green print:**
    - Cut 7 selvage-to-selvage strips 4³/₄"w. From these strips, cut 122 **rectangle E's** 4³/₄" x 2¹/₄".

4. **From pink print:**
    - Cut 2 selvage-to-selvage strips 7¹/₂"w. From these strips, cut 10 **square C's** 7¹/₂" x 7¹/₂".
    - Use **Template F** and follow **Template Cutting**, page 146, to cut 16 **F's**.

5. **From blue print:**
    - Cut 2 selvage-to-selvage strips 5"w. From these strips, cut 10 **square B's** 5" x 5".

6. **From pink solid:**
    - Cut 1 selvage-to-selvage strip 2"w. From this strip, cut 10 **square A's** 2" x 2".

PREPARING THE APPLIQUÉS

1. Use permanent fabric marker and patterns, pages 60 - 61, to trace 10 **A's**, 10 **B's**, 10 **C's**, 40 **D's**, and 122 **E's** onto stabilizer, leaving at least 1" between shapes. Cut out shapes, leaving approximately ¹/₂" around edges.

2. To make each appliqué, place 1 traced stabilizer piece on right side of matching fabric piece (*Example*: stabilizer **A** and fabric **square A**). Stitch pieces together directly on marked line. Trim fabric and stabilizer to within ¹/₄" of stitching line and clip curves and points. To make opening for turning, cut a slit through stabilizer only (**Fig. 1**). Turn right side out and press with dry iron. Make 10 **Appliqué A's**, 10 **Appliqué B's**, 10 **Appliqué C's**, and 122 **Appliqué E's**. Make 40 **Appliqué D's**, leaving bottom edge open for turning.

Fig. 1

Appliqué A (make 10)

Appliqué B (make 10)

Appliqué C (make 10)

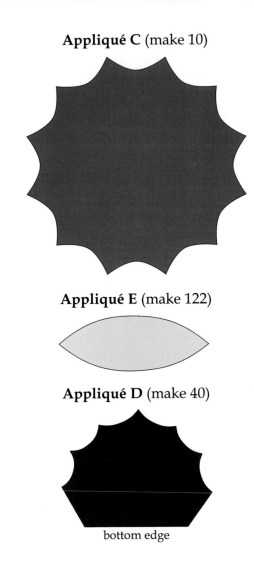

Appliqué E (make 122)

Appliqué D (make 40)

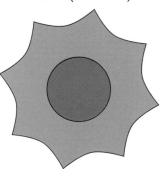

bottom edge

MAKING THE BLOCKS

Follow Mock Hand Appliqué, page 150, to stitch appliqués in place.

1. Stitch 1 **Appliqué A** to 1 **Appliqué B** to make **Unit 1**. Make 10 **Unit 1's**.

Unit 1 (make 10)

2. Stitch 1 **Unit 1** to **Appliqué C** to make **Unit 2**. Make 10 **Unit 2's**.

Unit 2 (make 10)

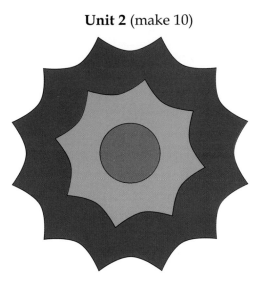

3. To make placement quidelines for appliqués, press 1 **background square** in half twice diagonally.
4. Referring to **Block** diagram, arrange 4 **Appliqué D's** and 1 **Unit 2** on **background square**, using pressed lines as guides. Pin **Appliqué D's** in place and set **Unit 2** aside. Stitch **Appliqué D's** to **background square**.
5. Reposition **Unit 2** on **background square** and stitch in place.
6. Referring to **Block** diagram, arrange 12 **Appliqué E's** on **background square** and stitch in place.
7. Follow manufacturer's instructions to remove remaining stabilizer from block.
8. Trim **background square** to 20$\frac{1}{2}$" x 20$\frac{1}{2}$" to complete **Block**.
9. Repeat Steps 3 - 8 to make a total of 9 **Blocks**.

Block (make 9)

ASSEMBLING THE QUILT TOP

*Follow **Piecing and Pressing**, page 146, to complete quilt top.*

1. To make placement guidelines for appliqués, press **pillow flip** in half from top to bottom and again from left to right.
2. Refer to **Quilt Top Diagram** and repeat Steps 4 - 7 of **Making the Blocks**, page 57, to stitch remaining **Appliqué D's**, **Unit 2**, and **Appliqué E's** to pillow flip.
3. Assemble 8 **F's** along long sides, starting and stopping stitching at dots (**Fig. 2**) to make **star**. Make 4 **stars**.

Fig. 2

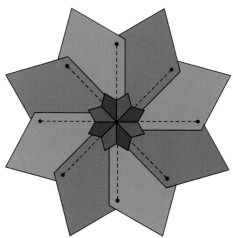

4. Cut 4 **squares** 8" x 8" from stabilizer. Place 1 stabilizer **square** on right side of 1 **star** and stitch pieces together ¼" from outer edges. Refer to Step 2 of **Preparing the Appliqués**, page 56, to trim and turn right side out to complete **Appliqué Star**. Make 4 **Appliqué Stars**.

Appliqué Star (make 4)

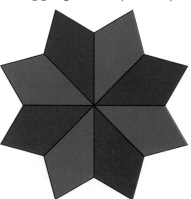

5. Referring to **Quilt Top Diagram**, assemble **Blocks** into rows. Sew rows together to make center section of quilt top.

6. Referring to **Quilt Top Diagram**, follow **Mock Hand Appliqué**, page 150, to stitch **Appliqué Stars** over corners of **Blocks** to complete center section of quilt top.
7. Follow **Adding Squared Borders**, page 151, to attach **side**, then **top** and **bottom inner borders**. Attach **pillow flip**, **bottom border**, then **side outer borders**.
8. Referring to photo and **Quilt Top Diagram**, use 4 strands of floss to work **Chain Stitch**, page 158, between **Applique E's** on **pillow flip** to complete **Quilt Top**.

COMPLETING THE QUILT

1. Follow **Quilting**, page 152, to mark, layer, and quilt, using **Quilting Diagram**, page 60, as a suggestion. Our quilt is hand quilted using feather and cable patterns.
2. Cut a 34" square of binding fabric. Follow **Binding**, page 155, to bind quilt using 2½"w bias binding with overlapped corners.

— QUICK TIP — — — — —

KEEPING A QUILT JOURNAL

Because of their beauty and durability, quilts are often handed down from one generation to the next. Unfortunately, however, information about the quiltmaker is often lost. You can make sure that there will always be a record of your quilts by keeping a quilt journal.

Your journal can be as simple or as detailed as you'd like. In a notebook or photo album (or a combination of the two), you can assemble an entry for each quilt that might include:

- *The name that you have given the quilt and the traditional name of the pattern used.*
- *The dates you began and completed the quilt.*
- *A photo of the quilt or even shots made while the quilt is in progress.*
- *The name of the recipient and occasion, if the quilt was made as a gift.*
- *Swatches of the fabrics used and any special notes about fiber content or care.*
- *Your notes or drawings made while designing and making the quilt.*
- *A narrative diary of your thoughts during the time the quilt is being made.*

Whatever you choose to include, you will find the journal both useful and enjoyable as you refer back to it in the future.

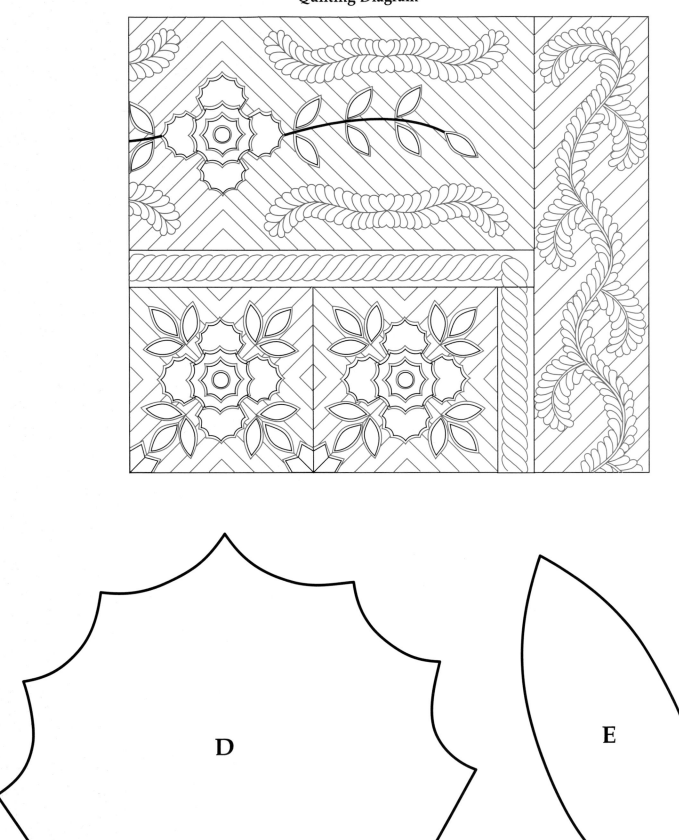

D

E

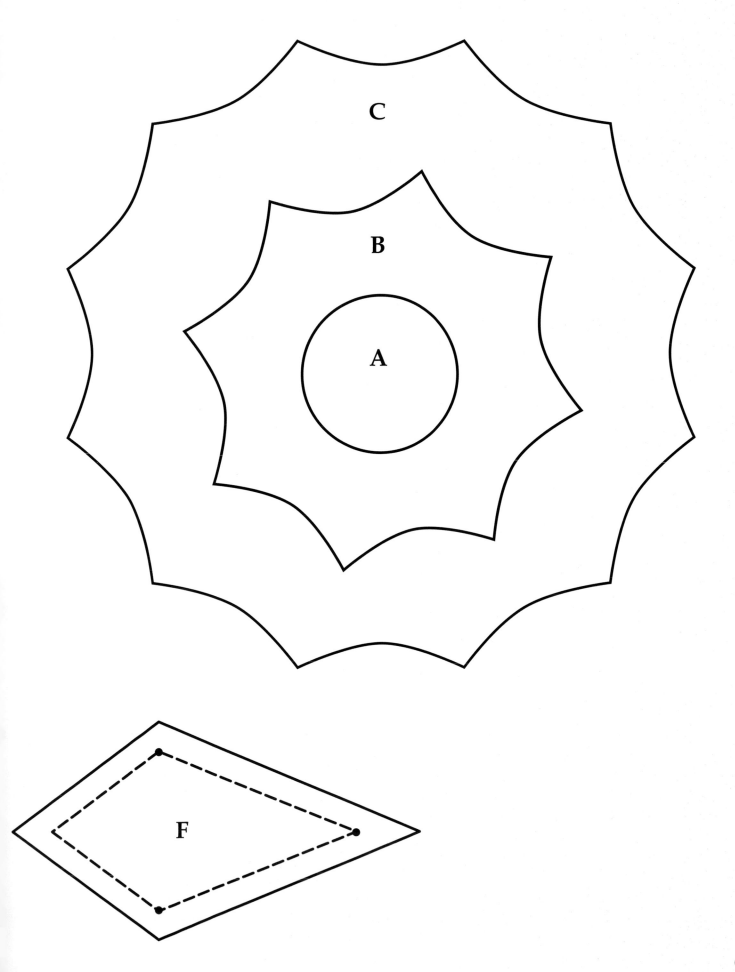

C

B

A

F

BABY BEAR COLLECTION

Not too hard, not too soft — our
Baby Bear crib quilt is just right for
a little one! The cuddly cub appliqués
are easy to create; just transfer the
bear pattern onto brown fabric and add
details with a fabric marker and paint.
Appliquéing the teddies in their "beds"
is just as simple to do using paper-backed
fusible web and clear nylon thread. The
soft-hued blankets, pillows, and sashing
strips are quick to strip piece and rotary
cut. The quilt is accented with bits of
lace and our hearts and ribbons quilting
pattern to ensure "beary" sweet dreams.

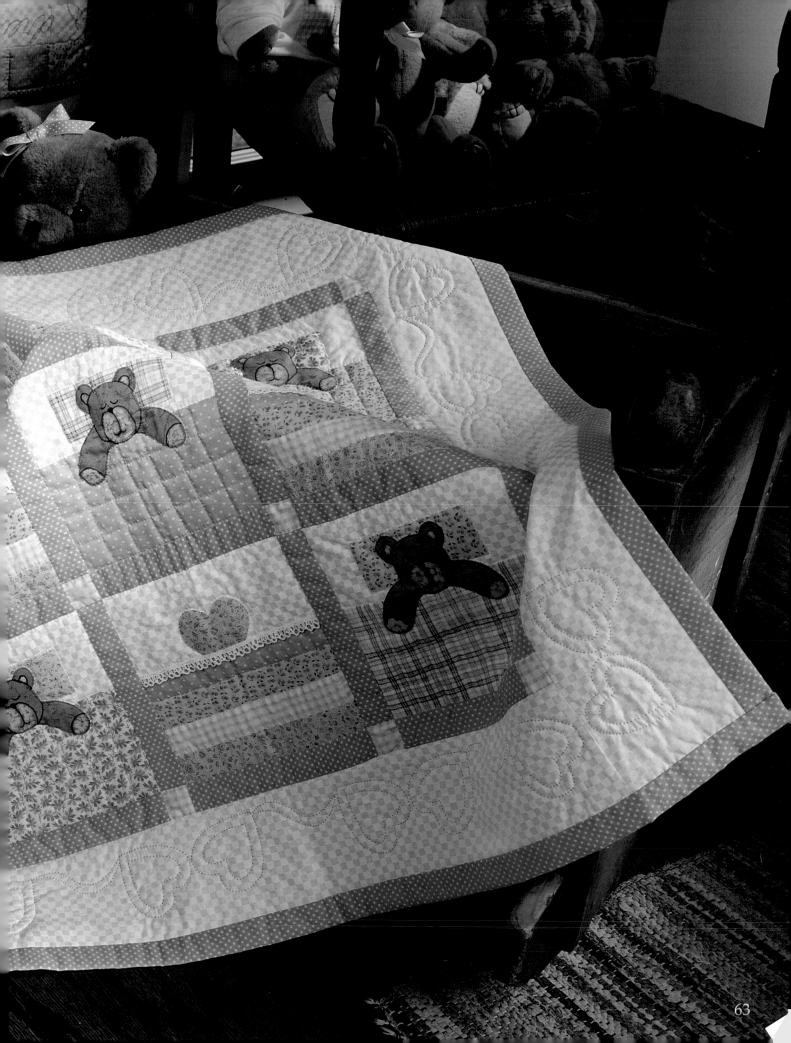

This appliquéd cub is snuggled in for a long, sweet slumber! The wall hanging (opposite) is easy to stitch using large rotary-cut shapes. You'll adore our nifty appliqué technique that makes it simple to secure the bear and pillow motifs, and the well-wishing message is fast to "stitch" using a permanent marker. Baby will be comfy and warm in this sweet sweatshirt (below). The machine-appliquéd design is accented with decorative blanket stitching.

BABY BEAR CRIB QUILT

SKILL LEVEL: 1 2 3 4 5
BLOCK SIZE: 7" x 7"
QUILT SIZE: 35" x 35"

YARDAGE REQUIREMENTS
Yardage is based on 45"w fabric.

- ☐ 7/8 yd of white check
- ■ 1/2 yd of blue dot
- ☐ 1/4 yd of yellow check
- ◩ 1/4 yd **each** of 5 pastel prints
- ▨ 1/4 yd of light brown print
  1 yd of 1/2"w flat lace trim
  1 1/4 yds for backing
  5/8 yd for binding
  45" x 60" batting

You will also need:

    paper-backed fusible web
    tracing paper
    iron-on transfer pen
    black permanent fabric marker
    cream fabric paint
    small paintbrush
    transparent monofilament thread for appliqué

CUTTING OUT THE PIECES
All measurements include a 1/4" seam allowance. Follow
Rotary Cutting, page 144, to cut fabric.

1. **From white check:** ☐
   - Cut 2 selvage-to-selvage strips 3 1/2"w. From these strips, cut 9 **rectangles** 3 1/2" x 7 1/2".
   - Cut 4 selvage-to-selvage strips 4 1/2"w. From these strips, cut 2 **top/bottom borders** 4 1/2" x 25 1/2" and 2 **side borders** 4 1/2" x 33 1/2".

2. **From blue dot:** ■
   - Cut 4 selvage-to-selvage strips 1 1/2"w. From these strips, cut 16 **sashing pieces** 1 1/2" x 7 1/2".
   - Cut 1 **large rectangle** 7 1/2" x 18".

3. **From yellow check:** ☐
   - Cut 1 selvage-to-selvage strip 1 1/2"w. Cut strip in half to make 2 **sashing strips**.

4. **From pastel prints and remaining yellow check:** ◩
   - Cut a total of 4 selvage-to-selvage **strips** 1 1/2"w for Heart Blocks.
   - Cut a total of 5 **blankets** 4 1/2" x 7 1/2".

5. **From flat lace trim:**
   - Cut 4 **lace pieces** 7 1/2"l.

PREPARING THE APPLIQUÉS

1. **To make pillows:** ◩
   - Follow **Preparing Appliqué Pieces**, page 149, to cut a total of 5 **pillows** 1 3/4" x 4 1/4" from pastel prints.

2. **To make hearts:** ▨
   - Use **Heart Pattern**, page 71, and follow **Preparing Appliqué Pieces**, page 149, to make 4 **hearts** from 1 pastel print.

3. **To make bears:** ▨
   - Follow **Preparing Appliqué Pieces**, page 149, to cut 5 rectangles 6" x 7" from light brown print.
   - Use transfer pen to trace **Bear Pattern**, page 71, onto tracing paper. Follow transfer pen manufacturer's instructions to transfer pattern to right side of each rectangle.
   - Referring to photo, use black fabric marker to darken inner detail lines on bears. Use paintbrush to dab cream paint on nose, paws, and inner ears.
   - Cut out **bears** along outer lines.

ASSEMBLING THE QUILT TOP
Follow Piecing and Pressing, page 146, to make quilt top.

1. Assemble 1 **rectangle** and 1 **blanket** to make **Unit 1**. Make 5 **Unit 1's**.

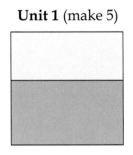

Unit 1 (make 5)

2. Assemble **strips** to make 1 **Strip Set A**. Cut across **Strip Set A** at 7 1/2" intervals to make 4 **Unit 2's**.

Strip Set A (make 1) **Unit 2** (make 4)

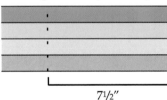

7 1/2"

3. Follow **Almost Invisible Appliqué**, page 149, to stitch **pillow** and **bear** to **Unit 1** to make **Bear Block**. Make 5 **Bear Blocks**.

Bear Block (make 5)

4. Follow **Almost Invisible Appliqué**, page 149, to stitch **hearts** to remaining **rectangles**, matching bottom edges of **hearts** and **rectangles**.

5. Assemble 1 **Unit 2** and 1 **rectangle**. Topstitch 1 **lace piece** along top of green strip to make **Heart Block**. Make 4 **Heart Blocks**.

Heart Block (make 4)

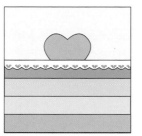

6. Assemble **large rectangle** and **sashing strips** to make 1 **Strip Set B** (ends will be uneven). Cut across **Strip Set B** at 1½" intervals to make 8 **Unit 4's**.

Strip Set B (make 1)   **Unit 4** (make 8)

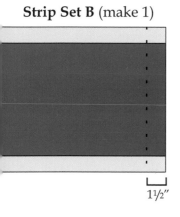

1½"

7. Assemble 2 **Unit 4's** and 1 **sashing piece** to make **Sashing Unit**. Make 4 **Sashing Units**.

Sashing Unit (make 4)

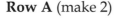

8. Assemble 4 **sashing pieces**, 2 **Bear Blocks**, and 1 **Heart Block** to make **Row A**. Make 2 **Row A's**.

Row A (make 2)

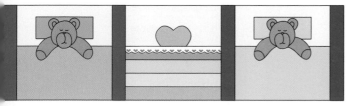

9. Assemble 4 **sashing pieces**, 2 **Heart Blocks**, and 1 **Bear Block** to make 1 **Row B**.

Row B (make 1)

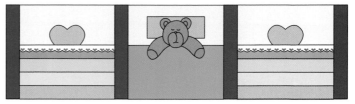

10. Referring to **Quilt Top Diagram**, assemble **Sashing Units**, **Row A's**, and **Row B** to complete center section of quilt top.

11. Attach **top**, **bottom**, then **side borders** to center section to complete **Quilt Top**.

COMPLETING THE QUILT

1. Follow **Quilting**, page 152, to mark, layer, and quilt, using **Quilting Diagram**, page 68, as a suggestion. Our quilt is hand quilted using **Border Quilting Pattern**, page 70.

2. Follow **Binding**, page 155, to bind quilt using 4½"w straight-grain binding with overlapped corners. When preparing quilt for binding, trim backing and batting a scant ¾" larger than quilt top.

Quilt Top Diagram

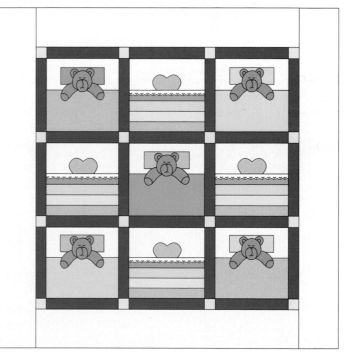

Quilting Diagram

"SWEET DREAMS" WALL HANGING

SKILL LEVEL: 1 2 3 4 5
WALL HANGING SIZE: 17" x 25"

YARDAGE REQUIREMENTS
Yardage is based on 45"w fabric.

 1/4 yd of white check
■ 1/4 yd of dark brown print
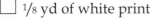 1/8 yd **each** of 6 pastel prints
□ 1/8 yd of white print
▦ scrap of light brown print
1/4 yd of 1/2"w flat lace trim
1/2 yd for backing and hanging sleeve
1/4 yd for binding
20" x 28" batting

You will also need:
paper-backed fusible web
tracing paper
iron-on transfer pen
black and brown permanent fabric markers
cream fabric paint
2 brown 5/8" buttons
small paintbrush
transparent monofilament thread for appliqué

CUTTING OUT THE PIECES
*All measurements include a 1/4" seam allowance. Follow **Rotary Cutting**, page 144, to cut fabric unless otherwise indicated.*

1. **From white check:** ☐
    *   Cut 2 selvage-to-selvage strips 2 1/2" w. From these strips, cut 2 **top/bottom inner borders** 2 1/2" x 8 1/2" and 2 **side inner borders** 2 1/2" x 20 1/2".
    *   Follow **Preparing Appliqué Pieces**, page 149, to make 1 **pillow** 1 3/4" x 4 1/4".

2. **From dark brown print:** ■
    *   Cut 1 **headboard** 3 1/2" x 7 1/2".
    *   Cut 1 **footboard** 1 1/2" x 7 1/2".
    *   Cut 1 selvage-to-selvage strip 1"w. From this strip, cut 2 **bedposts** 1" x 16 1/2".

3. **From pastel prints:** ◩
    *   Cut a total of 6 **blanket pieces** 1 1/2" x 7 1/2".
    *   Cut a total of 4 strips 2 1/2" x 24". Cut across strips at 2 1/2" intervals to make 36 **squares** for pieced borders.

4. **From white print:** ☐
    *   Cut 1 **lower piece** 3 1/4" x 7 1/2".
    *   Cut 1 **middle piece** 1 1/2" x 7 1/2".
    *   Cut 1 **upper piece** 2 3/4" x 7 1/2".

5. **From light brown print:** ▦
    *   Follow Step 3 of **Preparing the Appliqués** for **Baby Bear Crib Quilt**, page 66, to make 1 **bear**.

ASSEMBLING THE WALL HANGING TOP
*Follow **Piecing and Pressing**, page 146, to make wall hanging top.*

1. Assemble **upper piece, headboard, middle piece, blanket pieces, footboard,** and **lower piece** to make **Center Panel**.

Center Panel

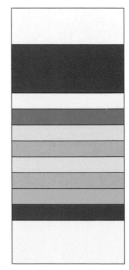

2. Sew lace across top of blue **blanket piece** and trim off excess. Sew **bedposts** to sides of **Center Panel**. Follow **Almost Invisible Appliqué**, page 149, to stitch **pillow** and **bear** in place to make **Bed Unit**.

Bed Unit

3. (*Note:* Refer to **Wall Hanging Top Diagram** for Steps 3 - 5.) Attach **top, bottom**, and then **side inner borders** to **Bed Unit** to make center section of wall hanging top.

4. Assemble 6 **squares** for each **top/bottom pieced border** and 12 **squares** for each **side pieced border**.

5. Attach **top, bottom**, then **side pieced borders** to center section to complete **Wall Hanging Top**.

COMPLETING THE WALL HANGING

1. Referring to photo, use **Sweet Dreams Pattern**, page 71, and brown fabric marker to trace words onto **inner borders**.

2. Follow **Quilting**, page 152, to mark, layer, and quilt, using **Quilting Diagram** as a suggestion. Our wall hanging is hand quilted.

3. Sew buttons to tops of **bedposts**.

4. Follow **Making a Hanging Sleeve**, page 157, to attach hanging sleeve to wall hanging back.

5. Follow **Binding**, page 155, to bind wall hanging using 2"w straight-grain binding with overlapped corners. When preparing wall hanging for binding, trim backing and batting even with wall hanging top.

Wall Hanging Top Diagram

Quilting Diagram

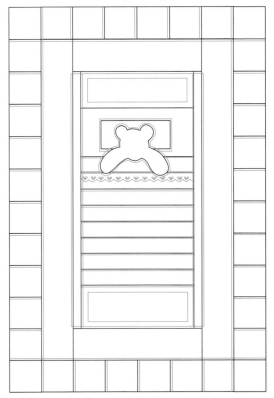

BABY BEAR SWEATSHIRT

SUPPLIES

- infant's white sweatshirt
- scraps of green, yellow, and light brown fabrics
- green and yellow embroidery floss
- paper-backed fusible web
- tracing paper
- iron-on transfer pen
- black permanent fabric marker
- cream fabric paint
- small paintbrush
- transparent monofilament thread for appliqué

MAKING THE SWEATSHIRT

1. Wash, dry, and press sweatshirt.
2. Use **Letter Pattern** and follow **Preparing Appliqué Pieces**, page 149, to make 1 **letter** from green and 1 **blanket** $3^1/4$" x $4^1/2$" from yellow.
3. Follow Step 3 of **Preparing the Appliqués** for **Baby Bear Crib Quilt**, page 66, to make 1 **bear** and 2 **feet**.
4. Referring to photo, fuse **blanket**, **letter**, **bear**, and **feet** to center front of sweatshirt.
5. Follow Steps 2 - 10 of **Almost Invisible Appliqué**, page 149, to stitch **bear** and **feet** to sweatshirt.
6. Using 4 strands of matching floss, work **Blanket Stitch**, page 158, along edges of **blanket** and **letter**.

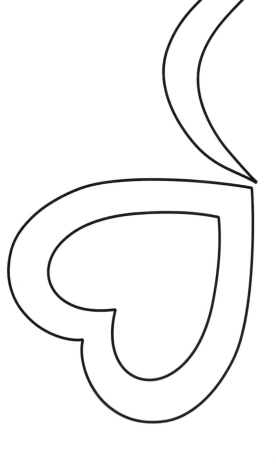

Border Quilting Pattern

Letter Pattern

Bear Pattern

Heart Pattern

Feet Pattern

Sweet Dreams Pattern

beary sweet dreams . . .

PATRIOTIC GEM

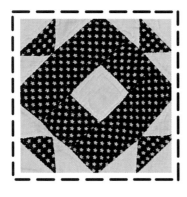

Quilters have long commemorated special events and displayed their patriotism through their handiwork. But at no other time did their zeal for quilting match their love of country than during the United States Centennial of 1876. Traditional pieced patterns and intricately appliquéd emblems were enthusiastically depicted in quilted designs — often in the red, white, and blue scheme that is still popular with quilters today. Our Patriotic Gem quilt celebrates that all-American spirit. Set off by plain red squares, each block is easy to make using strip piecing and a simple grid method for the triangle-squares. The quilt's old-fashioned charm is enhanced with a star-spangled inner border, along with outline, grid, and Baptist fan quilting.

PATRIOTIC GEM QUILT

SKILL LEVEL: 1 2 3 4 5
BLOCK SIZE: 6" x 6"
QUILT SIZE: 77" x 95"

Antique quilts are often too small to fit today's beds. Not only do our instructions include quick methods, but we've also resized our quilt to fit a full-size bed.

YARDAGE REQUIREMENTS
Yardage is based on 45"w fabric.

 3⅞ yds of blue print
■ 3¾ yds of red solid
□ 2¼ yds of white solid
7¼ yds for backing
¾ yd for binding
90" x 108" batting

CUTTING OUT THE PIECES
All measurements include a ¼" seam allowance. Follow Rotary Cutting, page 144, to cut fabric.

1. **From blue print:** ■
   • Cut 8 selvage-to-selvage **strips** 1⅞"w.
   • Cut 1 selvage-to-selvage strip 25"w. From this strip, cut 2 **large rectangles** 18" x 25" for triangle-squares.

large rectangle (cut 2)

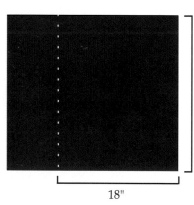

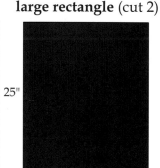

25"

18"

   • Cut 2 lengthwise strips 3½" x 88" for **side inner borders**.
   • Cut 2 lengthwise strips 3½" x 64" for **top/bottom inner borders**.
   • From remaining fabric, cut 26 crosswise strips 1⅞"w. From these strips, cut 130 **small rectangles** 1⅞" x 4¾".

small rectangle (cut 130)

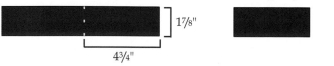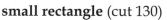

1⅞"

4¾"

2. **From red solid:**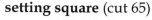
   • Cut 2 lengthwise strips 5½" x 98" for **side outer borders**.
   • Cut 2 lengthwise strips 5½" x 70" for **top/bottom outer borders**.
   • From remaining fabric, cut strips 6½"w. From these strips, cut a total of 65 **setting squares** 6½" x 6½".

setting square (cut 65)

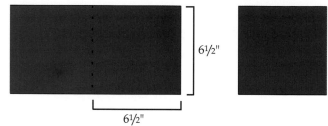

6½"

6½"

3. **From white solid:** □
   • Cut 4 selvage-to-selvage **strips** 2"w.
   • Cut 16 selvage-to-selvage strips 2⅜"w. From these strips, cut 260 squares 2⅜" x 2⅜". Cut squares once diagonally to make 520 **triangles**.

square (cut 260)   **triangle** (cut 520)

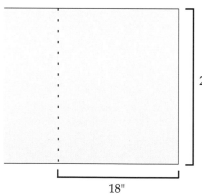

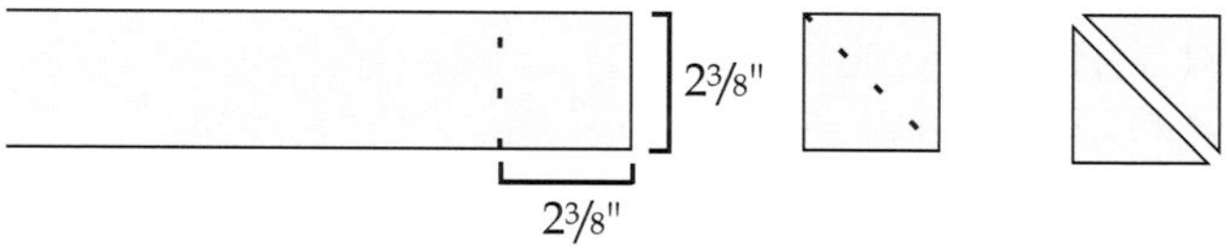

2⅜"

2⅜"

   • Cut 1 selvage-to-selvage strip 25"w. From this strip, cut 2 **large rectangles** 18" x 25" for triangle-squares.

large rectangle (cut 2)

25"

18"

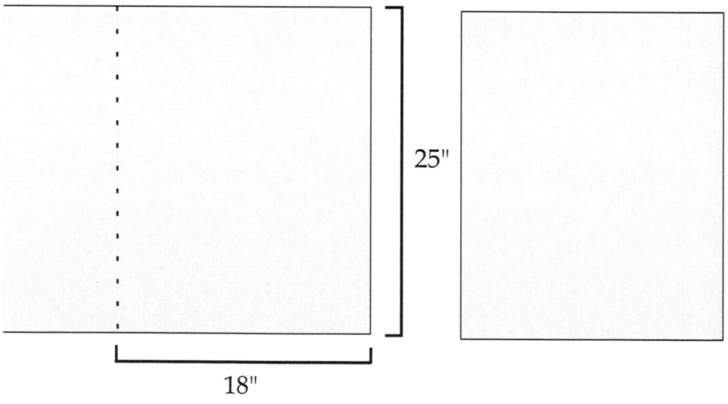

ASSEMBLING THE QUILT TOP

*Follow **Piecing and Pressing**, page 146, to make quilt top.*

1. Assemble **strips** to make **Strip Set**. Make 4 **Strip Sets**. Cut across **Strip Sets** at 2" intervals to make 65 **Unit 1's**.

Strip Set (make 4)   **Unit 1** (make 65)

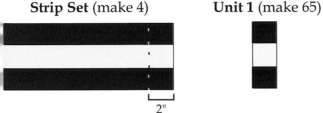

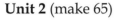

2. Assemble 2 **small rectangles** and 1 **Unit 1** to make **Unit 2**. Make 65 **Unit 2's**.

Unit 2 (make 65)

3. To make triangle-squares, place 1 white and 1 blue **large rectangle** right sides together. Referring to **Fig. 1**, follow Steps 1 - 3 of **Making Triangle-Squares**, page 147, to draw a grid of 70 squares 2³/₈" x 2³/₈". Referring to **Fig. 2** for stitching direction, follow Steps 4 - 6 of **Making Triangle-Squares** to complete 140 **triangle-squares**. Repeat with remaining **large rectangles** to make a total of 280 **triangle-squares** (you will need 260 and have 20 left over).

Fig. 1

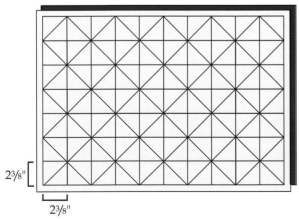

Fig. 2

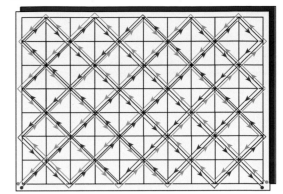

triangle-square (make 280)

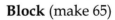

4. Assemble 1 **triangle-square** and 2 **triangles** to make **Unit 3**. Make 260 **Unit 3's**.

Unit 3 (make 260)

5. Assemble 4 **Unit 3's** and 1 **Unit 2** to make **Block**. Make 65 **Blocks**.

Block (make 65)

6. Assemble 5 **Blocks** and 5 **setting squares** to make **Row**. Make 13 **Rows**.

Row (make 13)

7. Referring to **Quilt Top Diagram**, assemble **Rows** to complete center section of quilt top.
8. Follow **Adding Squared Borders**, page 151, to attach **top**, **bottom**, and then **side inner borders** to center section of quilt top. Attach **top**, **bottom**, and then **side outer borders** to complete **Quilt Top**.

COMPLETING THE QUILT

1. Follow **Quilting**, page 152, to mark, layer, and quilt, using **Quilting Diagram** as a suggestion. Our quilt is hand quilted with Baptist fan designs on the borders.
2. For binding, cut 2¹/₂"w selvage-to-selvage strips from binding fabric; piece together to make a strip approximately 10¹/₄ yds long. Matching wrong sides and raw edges, press strip in half lengthwise. Follow **Attaching Binding with Mitered Corners**, page 156, to bind quilt.

Quilting Diagram

PARAMOUNT STAR

Many of the finest Colonial-era quilts were made in the medallion style, which features a large central design surrounded by a series of elaborate borders and enhanced with intricate quilting. To help simplify our Paramount Star quilt, we rotary cut many of the pieces, including the LeMoyne Star sections, and used a grid method for the Sawtooth borders. The sharp-pointed leaves on our appliquéd vines are easy to create with the help of water-soluble stabilizer, and machine blindstitch provides a faster way to achieve the look of hand appliqué. It's also easy to stitch perfect vines using a bias pressing bar — no more turning tubes inside out! A timeless design, this showpiece will be the star of your collection.

PARAMOUNT STAR QUILT

SKILL LEVEL: 1 2 3 4 5
QUILT SIZE: 98" x 111"

YARDAGE REQUIREMENTS

Yardage is based on 45"w fabric.

- ☐ 9³/₄ yds of white solid
- ■ 4¹/₈ yds of dark blue solid
- ■ 2³/₄ yds of blue print
- ■ 2¹/₈ yds of light blue solid
  8³/₄ yds for backing
  1 yd for binding
  120" x 120" batting

You will also need:
transparent monofilament thread for appliqué
2³/₈ yds of 19"w water-soluble stabilizer
³/₈" bias pressing bar

CUTTING OUT THE PIECES

All measurements include a ¼" seam allowance. Follow
Rotary Cutting, *page 144, to cut fabric unless otherwise
indicated. To simplify quilt top assembly, group all pieces
for each of the quilt sections listed into separate stacks.*

1.   From white solid: ☐

(for Feathered Star Medallion)
- Cut 1 **rectangle** 10" x 20" for triangle-squares.
- Cut 4 **medium squares** 2⁷/₈" x 2⁷/₈".
- Cut 2 squares 4⁵/₈" x 4⁵/₈". Cut squares twice diagonally to make 8 **medium triangles**.
- Cut 4 **large squares** 7³/₄" x 7³/₄".
- Cut 1 square 11¹/₂" x 11¹/₂". Cut square twice diagonally to make 4 **large triangles**.
- Cut 1 strip 2"w. From this strip, cut 8 squares 2" x 2". Cut each square once diagonally to make 16 **small triangles**.

(for Sawtooth Borders)
- Cut 13 **rectangles** 14" x 16" for triangle-squares.
- Cut 10 **squares** 1⁵/₈" x 1⁵/₈".

(for Vine Borders)
- Cut 4 selvage-to-selvage strips 6" x 41" for **inner vine borders**.
- Cut 2 lengthwise strips 6" x 82" for **top/bottom outer vine borders**.
- Cut 2 lengthwise strips 6" x 95" for **side outer vine borders**.

(for LeMoyne Star Blocks)
- Cut 2 selvage-to-selvage strips 2¹/₈"w. From these strips, cut 32 **small squares** 2¹/₈" x 2¹/₈".
- Cut 1 selvage-to-selvage strip 3¹/₂"w. From this strip, cut 8 squares 3¹/₂" x 3¹/₂". Cut each square twice diagonally to make 32 **small triangles**.
- Cut 7 selvage-to-selvage strips 3¹/₄"w. From these strips, cut 80 **medium squares** 3¹/₄" x 3¹/₄".
- Cut 3 selvage-to-selvage strips 5¹/₈"w. From these strips, cut 20 squares 5¹/₈" x 5¹/₈". Cut each square twice diagonally to make 80 **medium triangles**.

(for Setting Pieces)
- Cut 3 selvage-to-selvage strips 14³/₄"w. From these strips, cut 5 squares 14³/₄" x 14³/₄". Cut each square twice diagonally to make 20 **setting triangles** (you will need 18 and have 2 left over).
- Cut 2 squares 14³/₈" x 14³/₈". Cut each square once diagonally to make 4 **corner setting triangles**.

2.   From dark blue solid: ■

(for Feathered Star Medallion)
- Use **Template A** pattern, page 87, and follow **Template Cutting**, page 146, to cut 8 **A's**.

(for Sawtooth Borders)
- Cut 8 **rectangles** 14" x 16" for triangle-squares.

(for Vine Borders)
- Cut 1 **square** 27" x 27" for bias strip.
- Cut 3 selvage-to-selvage **strips** 4"w for leaf appliqués.

(for LeMoyne Star Blocks)
- Cut 4 selvage-to-selvage **strips** 1⁵/₈"w.
- Cut 16 selvage-to-selvage **strips** 2¹/₂"w.

3.   From blue print: ■

(for Feathered Star Medallion)
- Cut 1 selvage-to-selvage **strip** 2¹/₈"w.

(for Setting Pieces)
- Cut 2 squares 20" x 20". Cut each square once diagonally to make 4 **large triangles**.
- Cut 3 selvage-to-selvage strips 10"w. From these strips, cut 10 **setting squares** 10" x 10".
- Cut 2 selvage-to-selvage strips 14³/₄"w. From these strips, cut 4 squares 14³/₄" x 14³/₄". Cut each square twice diagonally to make 16 **setting triangles**.
- Cut 2 squares 7⁵/₈" x 7⁵/₈". Cut each square once diagonally to make 4 **small setting triangles**.

4.   From light blue solid: ■

(for Feathered Star Medallion)
- Cut 1 **rectangle** 10" x 20" for triangle-squares.
- Cut 1 selvage-to-selvage **strip** 1⁵/₈"w.

(for Sawtooth Borders)
- Cut 5 **rectangles** 14" x 16" for triangle-squares.

(for Vine Borders)
- Cut 1 **square** 18" x 18" for bias strip.
- Cut 2 selvage-to-selvage **strips** 4"w for leaf appliqués.

MAKING THE QUILT TOP SECTIONS

*Follow **Piecing and Pressing**, page 146, to make quilt top sections.*

FEATHERED STAR MEDALLION

1.   Referring to **Fig. 1**, align the 45° marking (shown in pink) on the rotary cutting ruler along the lower edge of light blue solid **strip**. Cut along right edge of ruler to cut 1 end of **strip** at a 45° angle.

Fig. 1

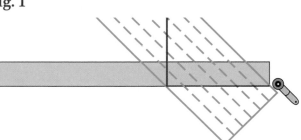

2. Turn cut strip 180° on mat and align the 45° marking on the rotary cutting ruler along the lower edge of the strip. Align the previously cut 45° edge with the 1⅝" marking on the ruler. Cut strip at 1⅝" intervals as shown in **Fig. 2** to cut a total of 8 **small diamonds**. Set aside for use in Step 12.

Fig. 2

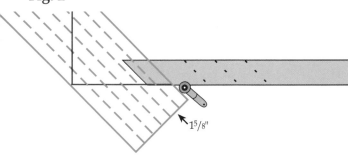

↖ 1⅝"

3. Using blue print **strip**, repeat Steps 1 and 2, cutting strip at 2⅛" intervals to make a total of 8 **large diamonds**.

4. Follow **Working with Diamond Shapes**, page 148, to assemble 8 **large diamonds**, 4 **medium squares**, and 4 **medium triangles** to make **Star Block**.

Star Block (make 1)

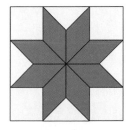

5. To make triangle-squares, place white solid and light blue solid **rectangles** right sides together and follow Steps 1 - 3 of **Making Triangle-Squares**, page 147, to draw a grid of 36 squares 2" x 2" (**Fig. 3**). Referring to **Fig. 3** for stitching direction, follow Steps 4 - 6 of **Making Triangle-Squares** to make a total of 72 **triangle-squares**.

Fig. 3

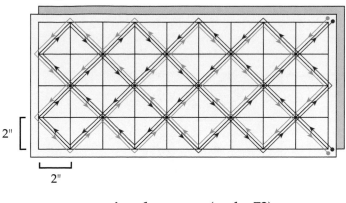

2"

2"

triangle-square (make 72)

6. Assemble 1 **small triangle** and 4 **triangle-squares** to make **Unit 1**. Make 4 **Unit 1's**.

Unit 1 (make 4)

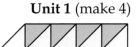

7. Assemble 1 **large triangle** and 1 **Unit 1** to make **Unit 2**, leaving portion of seam shown in pink unstitched at this time. Make 4 **Unit 2's**.

Unit 2 (make 4)

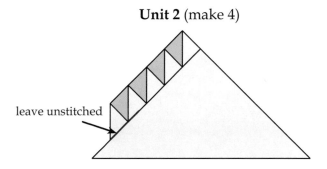

leave unstitched

8. Assemble 5 **triangle-squares** and 1 **small triangle** to make **Unit 3**. Make 4 **Unit 3's**.

Unit 3 (make 4)

9. Assemble 1 **Unit 2**, 1 **Unit 3**, and 1 **A** to make **Unit 4**, leaving portion of seam shown in pink unstitched at this time. Make 4 **Unit 4's**.

Unit 4 (make 4)

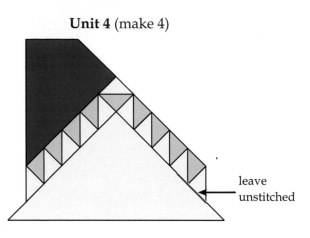

leave unstitched

10. Assemble 1 **A** and 1 **medium triangle** to make **Unit 5**. Make 4 **Unit 5's**.

Unit 5 (make 4)

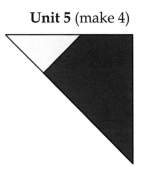

11. Assemble 1 **Unit 4** and 1 **Unit 5** to make **Unit 6**. Make 4 **Unit 6's**.

Unit 6 (make 4)

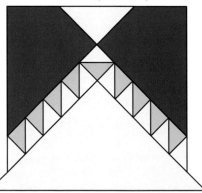

12. Assemble 1 **small diamond** and 1 **small triangle** to make **Unit 7**. Make 4 **Unit 7's**. Assemble 1 **small triangle** and 1 **small diamond** to make **Unit 8**. Make 4 **Unit 8's**.

Unit 7 (make 4)   **Unit 8** (make 4)

13. Assemble 1 **Unit 7** and 5 **triangle-squares** to make **Unit 9**. Make 4 **Unit 9's**.

Unit 9 (make 4)

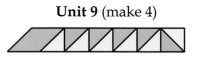

14. Assemble 4 **triangle-squares** and 1 **Unit 8** to make **Unit 10**. Make 4 **Unit 10's**.

Unit 10 (make 4)

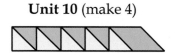

15. Assemble 1 **Unit 9**, 1 **Unit 10**, and 1 **large square** to make **Corner Block**. Make 4 **Corner Blocks**.

Corner Block (make 4)

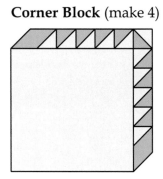

16. Assemble **Star Block**, **Unit 6's**, and **Corner Blocks** into rows (**Fig. 4**). Sew long seams to join rows, then finish sewing portions of seams left unstitched in Steps 7 and 9 to complete **Feathered Star Medallion**.

Fig. 4

SAWTOOTH BORDERS

1. To make triangle-squares, place 1 white solid and 1 light blue solid **rectangle** right sides together and follow Steps 1 - 3 of **Making Triangle-Squares**, page 147, to draw a grid of 42 squares 2" x 2" (**Fig. 5**). Referring to **Fig. 5** for stitching direction, follow Steps 4 - 6 of **Making Triangle-Squares** to make 84 triangle-squares. Repeat with remaining 4 light blue solid **rectangles** and 4 of the white **rectangles** to make a total of 420 **triangle-square A's** (you will need 414 and have 6 left over).

Fig. 5

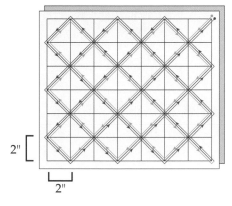

2"

2"

triangle-square A (make 420)

2. Repeat Step 1 using 8 white solid and 8 dark blue solid **rectangles** to make 672 **triangle-square B's**.

triangle-square B (make 672)

3. Referring to **Quilt Top Diagram**, page 86, for arrangement of **triangle-squares** and **squares**, assemble the numbers of pieces indicated in the **Sawtooth Border Assembly** table to make **Sawtooth Borders**.

VINE BORDERS

1. To make **Vine Appliqués**, use light blue solid **square** and follow Steps 1 - 7 of **Making Continuous Bias Strip Binding**, page 155, to make a 1¼"w bias strip. Cut bias strip into 4 pieces approximately 50"l. Use dark blue solid **square** to make a 1¼"w bias strip. Cut bias strip into 2 pieces approximately 100"l and 2 pieces approximately 110"l.

Sawtooth Border Assembly

Name of Border	Number of Borders to Make	Number of Pieces per Border	
		Triangle-Squares	Squares
1st (Inner) Side	2	22A	—
1st Top/Bottom	2	23A	1
2nd Side	2	34A	—
2nd Top/Bottom	2	34A	2
3rd Side	2	46A	—
3rd Top/Bottom	2	48A	—
4th Side	2	82B	—
4th Top/Bottom	2	72B	2
5th Side	2	96B	—
5th Top/Bottom	2	86B	—

2. Fold 1 bias strip in half lengthwise with wrong sides together; do not press. Stitch ¼" from long raw edge to form a tube; trim seam allowance to ⅛". Repeat with remaining bias strips.
3. Place bias pressing bar inside 1 bias tube. Center seam and press as you move bar down length of tube. Repeat with remaining bias tubes to complete **Vine Appliqués**.
4. To make **Leaf Appliqués**, cut 5 strips of stabilizer 4" x 42". Use a permanent fabric marker to trace **Leaf** pattern, page 87, onto stabilizer strips, leaving at least ½" between leaves. Place stabilizer strips on right side of 4"w fabric **strips**. Stitch on marked lines. Trim fabric and stabilizer to within ¼" of stitching line; clip curves and points. To make opening for turning, cut a slit through stabilizer only. Turn right side out and press with a dry iron. Make 36 light blue solid and 76 dark blue solid **Leaf Appliqués**.
5. Referring to **Quilt Top Diagram**, page 86, for placement, follow **Mock Hand Appliqué**, page 150, to stitch **Vine** and **Leaf Appliqués** to **inner** and **outer vine borders**.

LeMOYNE STAR BLOCKS

1. Using 1⅝"w **strips** and cutting at 1⅝" intervals, follow Steps 1 and 2 of **Feathered Star Medallion**, page 80, to cut 64 **diamonds**. Use **diamonds**, **small squares**, and **small triangles** and follow Step 4 of **Feathered Star Medallion**, page 81, to make 8 **Small Star Blocks**.
2. Using 2½"w **strips** and cutting at 2½" intervals, follow Steps 1 and 2 of **Feathered Star Medallion**, page 80, to cut 160 **diamonds**. Use **diamonds**, **medium squares**, and **medium triangles** and follow Step 4 of **Feathered Star Medallion**, page 81, to make 20 **Large Star Blocks**.

ASSEMBLING THE QUILT TOP

*Follow **Piecing and Pressing**, page 146, to make quilt top.*

1. (*Note:* Refer to **Center Medallion Diagram** for Steps 1 - 4.) Sew **1st Side Sawtooth Borders**, then **1st Top** and **Bottom Sawtooth Borders** to **Feathered Star Medallion**. Sew **large triangles** to sides of medallion.

Center Medallion Diagram

2. Sew **2nd Side Sawtooth Borders**, then **2nd Top** and **Bottom Sawtooth Borders** to medallion.
3. Sew 1 **Small Star Block** to each end of **top** and **bottom inner vine borders**. Sew **side**, then **top** and **bottom inner vine borders** to medallion.
4. Sew **3rd Side Sawtooth Borders**, then **3rd Top** and **Bottom Sawtooth Borders** to medallion to complete **Center Medallion**.
5. Assemble 2 **small setting triangles**, 3 blue print **setting triangles**, 4 **Large Star Blocks**, 3 **setting squares**, and 2 white **setting triangles** to make **Unit 11**. Make 2 **Unit 11's**.

Unit 11 (make 2)

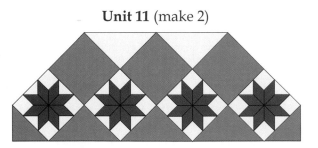

6. Assemble 5 blue print **setting triangles**, 4 **Large Star Blocks**, and 3 white **setting triangles** to make **Unit 12**. Make 2 **Unit 12's**.

Unit 12 (make 2)

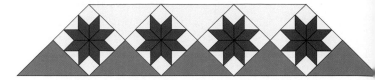

7. Assemble 1 **setting square**, 1 **Large Star Block**, 2 white **setting triangles**, and 1 **corner setting triangle** to make **Unit 13**. Make 2 **Unit 13's**.

Unit 13 (make 2)

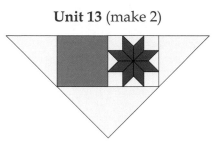

8. Assemble 1 **Large Star Block**, 1 **setting square**, 2 white **setting triangles**, and 1 **corner setting triangle** to make **Unit 14**. Make 2 **Unit 14's**.

Unit 14 (make 2)

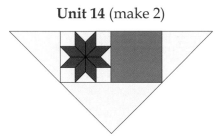

9. Referring to **Assembly Diagram**, sew **Unit 11's** to top and bottom of **Center Medallion**. Add **Unit 12's** to sides, then **Unit 13's** and **Unit 14's** to appropriate corners to complete center section of quilt top.

Assembly Diagram

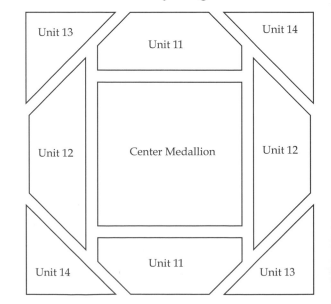

10. (*Note:* Refer to **Quilt Top Diagram**, page 86, when adding remaining borders.) Sew **4th Side Sawtooth Borders**, then **4th Top** and **Bottom Sawtooth Borders** to center section of quilt top.

11. Sew 1 **Small Star Block** to each end of **top** and **bottom outer vine borders**. Sew **side**, then **top** and **bottom outer vine borders** to center section of quilt top.

12. Sew **5th Side Sawtooth Borders**, then **5th Top** and **Bottom Sawtooth Borders** to center section of quilt top to complete **Quilt Top**.

COMPLETING THE QUILT

1. Follow **Quilting**, page 152, to mark, layer, and quilt, using **Quilting Diagram** as a suggestion. Our quilt is hand quilted using classic feather, feather wreath, and shell designs.

2. Cut a 36" square of binding fabric. Follow **Binding**, page 155, to bind quilt using 2½"w bias binding with mitered corners.

Quilting Diagram

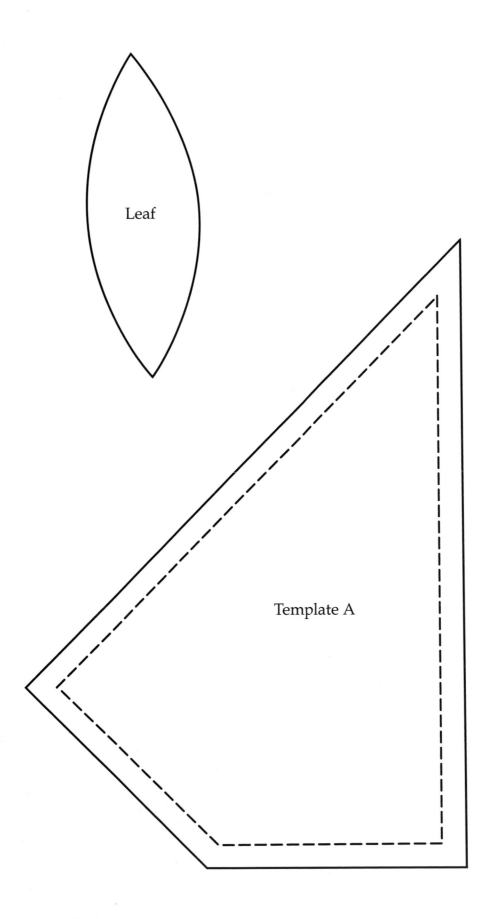

Leaf

Template A

SCHOOLHOUSE COLLECTION

Originating in the mid-1800's, the Schoolhouse pattern was inspired by the charming one-room schools commonly found throughout rural America. Just as quilters of the 1920's and 1930's rediscovered the design's timeless appeal, you'll also love the simple nostalgia of our Schoolhouse quilt. Each block is easily assembled in sections using strip-cut units and pieces cut from basic template shapes. Complementing the pattern are bold sashing strips and setting squares that are created with easy rotary-cutting and strip-piecing techniques. Clever outline quilting provides an A$^+$ finish.

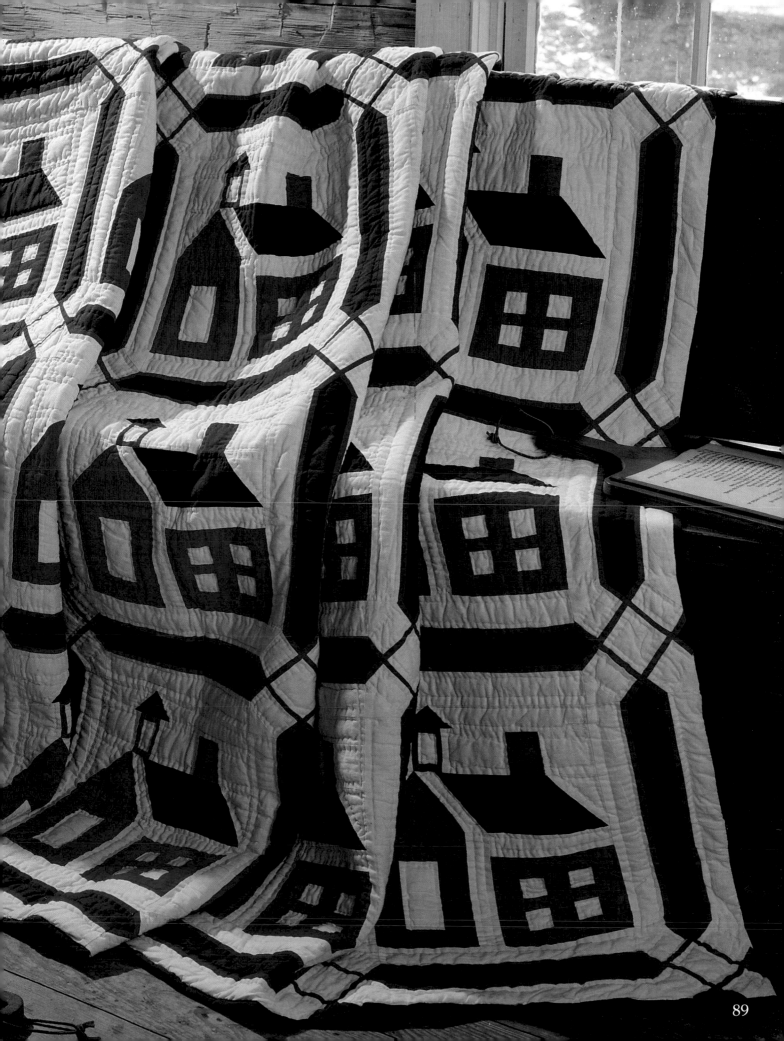

These coordinating accessories (below) really make the grade! The Schoolhouse quilt block becomes a quaint pillow when bordered with a variety of plaid fabrics and button-topped stars. For our alphabet pillow, you'll learn that "A" is for apple — and appliqué, too. It's easy to secure the appealing motifs using paper-backed fusible web and clear nylon thread. Teacher will award a gold star for this smart wall hanging (opposite). A patchwork and appliqué primer, the piece includes a valuable lesson that's "stitched" with a permanent pen.

SCHOOLHOUSE QUILT

SKILL LEVEL: 1 2 3 **4** 5
BLOCK SIZE: 11½" x 11½"
QUILT SIZE: 88" x 105"

YARDAGE REQUIREMENTS
Yardage is based on 45"w fabric.

 7 yds of cream solid
■ 4½ yds of red solid
■ 2⅞ yds of blue solid
8¼ yds for backing
1 yd for binding
120" x 120" batting

CUTTING OUT THE PIECES
All measurements include a ¼" seam allowance. Follow
***Rotary Cutting**, page 144, to cut fabric unless otherwise
indicated. Label each set of cut pieces for easy identification.*

1. **From cream solid:** □
(for Schoolhouse Blocks)
   - Cut 3 selvage-to-selvage **B strips** 2¼"w.
   - Cut 5 selvage-to-selvage strips 1½"w. From these strips, cut 30 **D's** 1½" x 6".
   - Cut 6 selvage-to-selvage **H strips** 1⅜"w.
   - Cut 5 selvage-to-selvage strips 1⅝"w. From these strips, cut 30 **I's** 1⅝" x 6½".
   - Cut 4 selvage-to-selvage **N strips** 2¾"w.
   - Cut 2 selvage-to-selvage **P strips** 2"w.
   - Cut 2 selvage-to-selvage **Q strips** 4⅜"w.
   - Cut 3 selvage-to-selvage strips 1¾"w. From these strips, cut 30 **S's** 1¾" x 3½".
   - Cut 8 selvage-to-selvage strips 1¾"w. From these strips, cut 30 **U's** 1¾" x 9".
   - Use patterns **J** and **L**, page 98, and follow **Template Cutting**, page 146, to cut 60 **J's** (30 in reverse) and 30 **L's**.

(for Sashing)
   - Cut 48 selvage-to-selvage **AA strips** 2"w.
   - Cut 6 selvage-to-selvage **DD strips** 1⅝"w.
   - Cut 7 selvage-to-selvage **EE strips** 2⅝"w.
   - Cut 5 selvage-to-selvage strips 2⅜"w. From these strips, cut 84 squares 2⅜" x 2⅜". Cut squares once diagonally to make 168 triangle **GG's**.

2. **From red solid:** ■
(for Schoolhouse Blocks)
   - Cut 6 selvage-to-selvage **A strips** 1⅞"w.
   - Cut 8 selvage-to-selvage strips 1⅝"w. From these strips, cut 60 **C's** 1⅝" x 5".
   - Cut 12 selvage-to-selvage strips 1¾"w. From these strips, cut 90 **E's** 1¾" x 4⅞".
   - Cut 6 selvage-to-selvage **F strips** 1½"w.
   - Cut 3 selvage-to-selvage **G strips** 1⅛"w.

   - Cut 3 selvage-to-selvage strips 3¼"w. From these strips, use pattern **K**, page 99, and follow **Template Cutting**, page 146, to cut 30 **K's**.
   - Cut 8 selvage-to-selvage **O strips** ¾"w.
   - Cut 2 selvage-to-selvage **R strips** 2⅛"w.

(for Sashing)
   - Cut 62 selvage-to-selvage **BB strips** ¾"w.
   - Cut 12 selvage-to-selvage strips ¾"w. From these strips, cut 84 **HH's** ¾" x 5½".

3. **From blue solid:** ■
(for Schoolhouse Blocks)
   - Cut 6 selvage-to-selvage strips 3¼"w. From these strips, use pattern **M**, page 98, and follow **Template Cutting**, page 146, to cut 30 **M's**.
   - Cut 3 selvage-to-selvage strips 1¾"w. From these strips, cut 30 **T's** 1¾" x 3".

(for Sashing)
   - Cut 24 selvage-to-selvage **CC strips** 2"w.
   - Cut 8 selvage-to-selvage **FF strips** 1⅝"w.

ASSEMBLING THE QUILT TOP
*Follow **Piecing and Pressing**, page 146, to make quilt top.*

MAKING THE BLOCKS
1. Assemble 2 **A strips** and 1 **B strip** to make **Strip Set A**. Make 3 **Strip Set A's**. Cut across strip sets at 3¾" intervals to make 30 **Unit 1's**.

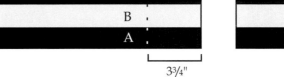

Strip Set A (make 3)   Unit 1 (make 30)

2. Assemble 2 **C's**, 1 **Unit 1**, and 1 **D** to make **Unit 2**. Make 30 **Unit 2's**.

Unit 2 (make 30)

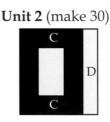

3. Assemble 2 **F strips**, 2 **H strips**, and 1 **G strip** to make **Strip Set B**. Make 3 **Strip Set B's**. Cut across strip sets at 1⅝" intervals to make 60 **Unit 3's**.

Strip Set B (make 3)   Unit 3 (make 60)

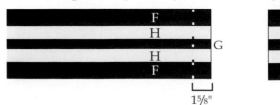

4. Assemble 3 **E's**, 2 **Unit 3's**, and 1 **I** to make **Unit 4**. Make 30 **Unit 4's**.

Unit 4 (make 30)

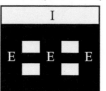

5. Assemble 1 **J**, 1 **K**, 1 **L**, 1 **M**, and 1 reverse **J** to make **Unit 5**. Make 30 **Unit 5's**.

Unit 5 (make 30)

6. Assemble 1 **N strip** and 1 **O strip** to make **Strip Set C**. Make 2 **Strip Set C's**. Cut across strip sets at 2½" intervals to make 30 **Unit 6's**.

Strip Set C (make 2)　　**Unit 6** (make 30)

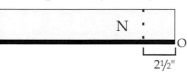

7. Assemble 2 **O strips** and 1 **P strip** to make **Strip Set D**. Make 2 **Strip Set D's**. Cut across strip sets at 1½" intervals to make 30 **Unit 7's**.

Strip Set D (make 2)　　**Unit 7** (make 30)

8. Assemble 1 **O strip**, 1 **Q strip**, 1 **R strip**, and 1 **N strip** to make **Strip Set E**. Make 2 **Strip Set E's**. Cut across strip sets at 2½" intervals to make 30 **Unit 8's**.

Strip Set E (make 2)　　**Unit 8** (make 30)

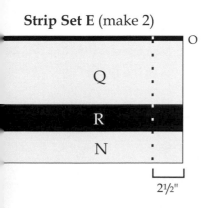

9. Assemble 1 **Unit 6**, 1 **Unit 7**, and 1 **Unit 8** to make **Unit 9**. Make 30 **Unit 9's**.

Unit 9 (make 30)

10. Place 1 **S** on 1 **T** as shown in **Fig. 1** and stitch diagonally. Trim ¼" from stitching line (**Fig. 2**) and press open. Place 1 **U** on **T** (**Fig. 3**) and stitch diagonally. Trim ¼" from stitching and press open to make **Unit 10**. Make 30 **Unit 10's**.

Fig. 1　　　**Fig. 2**　　　**Fig. 3**

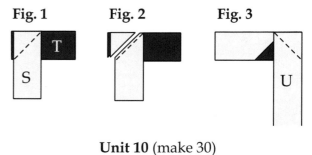

Unit 10 (make 30)

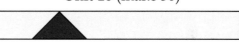

11. Assemble 1 **Unit 2**, 1 **Unit 4**, 1 **Unit 5**, 1 **Unit 9** and 1 **Unit 10** to complete **Block**. Make 30 **Blocks**.

Block (make 30)

MAKING THE SASHING

1. Assemble 2 **AA strips**, 2 **BB strips**, and 1 **CC strip** to make **Sashing Strip Set**. Make 24 **Sashing Strip Sets**. Cut across strip sets at 12" intervals to make 71 **Sashing Units**.

Sashing Strip Set (make 24)　　**Sashing Unit** (make 71)

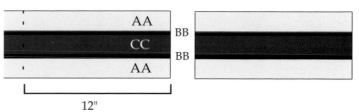

2. Assemble 2 **DD strips**, 2 **BB strips**, and 1 **EE strip** to make **Strip Set F**. Make 3 **Strip Set F's**. Cut across strip sets at 2⅝" intervals to make 42 **Unit 11's**.

Strip Set F (make 3)   **Unit 11** (make 42)

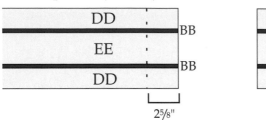

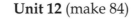
2⅝"

3. Assemble 2 **FF strips**, 2 **BB strips**, and 1 **EE strip** to make **Strip Set G**. Make 4 **Strip Set G's**. Cut across strip sets at 1⅝" intervals to make 84 **Unit 12's**.

Strip Set G (make 4)   **Unit 12** (make 84)

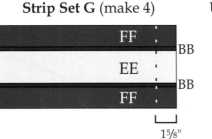

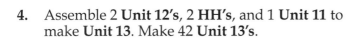
1⅝"

4. Assemble 2 **Unit 12's**, 2 **HH's**, and 1 **Unit 11** to make **Unit 13**. Make 42 **Unit 13's**.

Unit 13 (make 42)

5. Assemble 4 **GG's** and 1 **Unit 13**, centering **GG's** as shown in **Fig. 4**; press open. Trim as shown in **Fig. 5**, lining up edge of ruler with outer edges of **GG's** to complete **Sashing Block**. Make 42 **Sashing Blocks**.

Fig. 4   **Fig. 5**

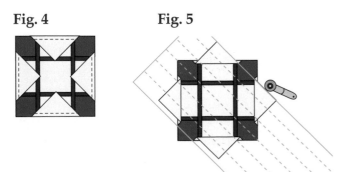

Sashing Block (make 42)

ASSEMBLING THE QUILT TOP

1. Assemble 6 **Sashing Blocks** and 5 **Sashing Units** to make **Row A**. Make 7 **Row A's**.

Row A (make 7)

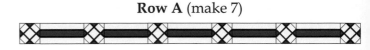

2. Assemble 6 **Sashing Units** and 5 **Blocks** to make **Row B**. Make 6 **Row B's**.

Row B (make 6)

3. Referring to **Quilt Top Diagram**, assemble **Row A's** and **Row B's** to complete **Quilt Top**.

COMPLETING THE QUILT

1. Follow **Quilting**, page 152, to mark, layer, and quilt, using **Quilting Diagram** as a suggestion. Our quilt is hand quilted.

2. Cut a 34" square of binding fabric. Follow **Binding**, page 155, to bind quilt using 2½"w bias binding with mitered corners.

Quilting Diagram

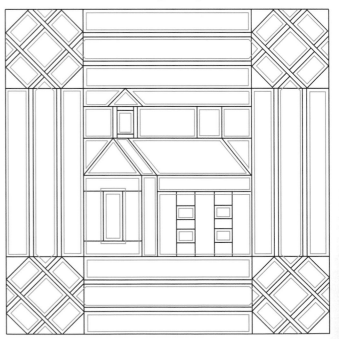

Quilt Top Diagram

SCHOOLHOUSE PILLOW

PILLOW SIZE: 16" x 16"

YARDAGE REQUIREMENTS
Yardage is based on 45"w fabric.

☐ 1/4 yd of cream print

■ 1/4 yd of red print

■ 1/8 yd **each** of 4 red and 4 blue plaids for borders

◨ gold and blue scraps
  20" x 20" pillow top backing
  1/4 yd for binding
  151/2" x 151/2" pillow back
  20" x 20" batting

You will also need:
  polyester fiberfill
  transparent monofilament thread for appliqué
  paper-backed fusible web
  4 blue 1/2" buttons

CUTTING OUT THE PIECES
All measurements include a 1/4" seam allowance. Follow Rotary Cutting, page 144, to cut fabric unless otherwise indicated. Label pieces for easy identification.

1. From cream print: ☐
  • Cut 1 **B** 21/4" x 33/4".
  • Cut 1 **D** 11/2" x 6".
  • Cut 2 **H's** 13/8" x 6".
  • Cut 1 **I** 15/8" x 61/2".

  • Use patterns **J** and **L**, page 98, and follow **Template Cutting**, page 146, to cut 2 **J's** (1 in reverse) and 1 **L**.
  • Cut 2 **N's** 21/2" x 23/4".
  • Cut 1 **P** 11/2" x 2".
  • Cut 1 **Q** 21/2" x 43/8".
  • Cut 1 **S** 13/4" x 31/2".
  • Cut 1 **U** 13/4" x 9".

2. From red print: ■
  • Cut 2 **A's** 17/8" x 33/4".
  • Cut 2 **C's** 15/8" x 5".
  • Cut 3 **E's** 13/4" x 47/8".
  • Cut 2 **F's** 11/2" x 6".
  • Cut 1 **G** 11/8" x 6".
  • Use pattern **K**, page 99, and follow **Template Cutting**, page 146, to cut 1 **K**.
  • Cut 2 **O's** 3/4" x 21/2".
  • Cut 1 **R** 21/8" x 21/2".
  • Cut 2 **W's** 3/4" x 11/2".

3. From red and blue plaids: ◨
  • Use pattern **M**, page 98, and follow **Template Cutting**, page 146, to cut 1 **M**.
  • Using a different fabric for each piece, cut:
    2 **top/bottom inner borders** 11/4" x 12"
    2 **side inner borders** 11/4" x 131/2"
    2 **top/bottom outer borders** 11/2" x 131/2"
    2 **side outer borders** 11/2" x 151/2".

4. From gold and blue scraps: ◨
  • From gold, use **Small Star** pattern, page 100, and follow **Preparing Appliqué Pieces**, page 149, to make 4 **Small Stars**.
  • From blue, cut 1 **T** 13/4" x 3".

ASSEMBLING THE PILLOW TOP
Follow Piecing and Pressing, page 146, to make pillow top.

1. (*Note:* Refer to **Block** diagram, page 96, for Steps 1 - 7 to make Block.) Assemble **A's**, **B**, **C's**, and **D** to make **Unit 1**.
2. Assemble **F's**, **G**, and **H's** to make 1 **Strip Set**. Cut across **Strip Set** at 15/8" intervals to make 2 **Unit 2's**.

Strip Set (make 1) **Unit 2** (make 2)

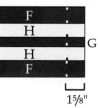

3. Assemble **Unit 2's**, **E's**, and **I** to make **Unit 3**.
4. Assemble **J**, **K**, **L**, **M**, and reverse **J** to make **Unit 4**.
5. Assemble **N's**, **O's**, **P**, **W's**, **Q**, and **R** to make **Unit 5**.

6. Use **S**, **T**, and **U** and follow Step 10 of **Assembling the Quilt Top for Schoolhouse Quilt**, page 93, to make **Unit 6**.
7. Assemble **Units 1**, **3**, **4**, **5**, and **6** to complete **Block**.

Block

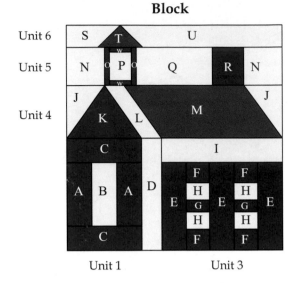

Unit 6
Unit 5
Unit 4

Unit 1   Unit 3

8. Attach **top**, **bottom**, then **side inner borders** to **Block**. Repeat with **outer borders**.
9. Refer to photo and follow **Almost Invisible Appliqué**, page 149, to stitch **Small Stars** to corners of inner borders to complete **Pillow Top**.

COMPLETING THE PILLOW

1. Follow **Quilting**, page 152, to mark, layer, and quilt, using **Quilting Diagram** as a suggestion. Our pillow top is machine quilted.
2. Sew buttons to stars.
3. Follow Steps 2 - 5 of **Completing the Pillow** for **Alphabet Pillow** to complete pillow.

Quilting Diagram

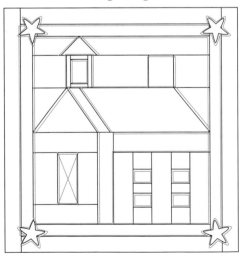

ALPHABET PILLOW

PILLOW SIZE: 15" x 15"

YARDAGE REQUIREMENTS

Yardage is based on 45"w fabric.

3/8 yd of cream print
1/4 yd of blue plaid
1/8 yd of gold print
scraps for apple and alphabet appliqués
19" x 19" pillow top backing
1/4 yd for binding
14 1/2" x 14 1/2" pillow back
19" x 19" batting

You will also need:
polyester fiberfill
transparent monofilament thread for appliqué
paper-backed fusible web

MAKING THE PILLOW TOP

All measurements include a 1/4" seam allowance. Follow Piecing and Pressing, page 146, to make pillow top.

1. Follow **Rotary Cutting**, page 144, to cut the following pieces:
   • 1 **background square** 9 1/2" x 9 1/2" from cream print.
   • 2 **top/bottom inner borders** 1 1/4" x 9 1/2" and 2 **side inner borders** 1 1/4" x 11" from gold print.
   • 2 **top/bottom outer borders** 2 1/4" x 11" and 2 **side outer borders** 2 1/4" x 14 1/2" from blue plaid.
2. Referring to photo, use **Apple** and **Pillow Alphabet** patterns, page 99, and follow **Preparing Appliqué Pieces**, page 149, to cut **appliqué pieces** from scraps.
3. Follow **Almost Invisible Appliqué**, page 149, to stitch **appliqué pieces** to **background square**.
4. Attach **top**, **bottom**, then **side inner borders** to **background square**. Repeat with **outer borders** to complete **Pillow Top**.

COMPLETING THE PILLOW

1. Follow **Quilting**, page 152, to mark, layer, and quilt. Our pillow top is machine quilted in the ditch along seamlines and appliqué edges; diagonal lines are stitched on outer border (see photo).
2. Place pillow back and pillow top wrong sides together. Using a 1/4" seam allowance, sew pillow back and top together, leaving an opening on 1 side for stuffing.
3. Stuff pillow with fiberfill and sew opening closed.
4. Follow **Binding**, page 155, to make 2 1/4 yds of 2 1/2"w straight-grain binding.
5. Follow **Attaching Binding with Mitered Corners**, page 156, to attach binding to pillow.

SCHOOL DAYS WALL HANGING

SKILL LEVEL: 1 2 3 4 5
WALL HANGING SIZE: 31" x 30"

YARDAGE REQUIREMENTS

Yardage is based on 45"w fabric.

- ½ yd of blue plaid for outer borders
- ½ yd **total** of assorted cream prints
- ¼ yd of gold print for inner borders
- scraps of assorted blue, red, green, and gold prints and white solid
- 1 yd for backing
- ¼ yd for binding
- 45" x 60" batting

You will also need:

1 pieced Schoolhouse Block (follow **Schoolhouse Pillow**, page 95, through Step 7 of Assembling the Pillow Top, omitting borders and appliqués)
transparent monofilament thread for appliqué
paper-backed fusible web
2 blue ½" buttons
black permanent fabric marker

CUTTING OUT THE PIECES

All measurements include a ¼" seam allowance. Follow Rotary Cutting, page 144, to cut fabric.

- **From blue plaid for outer borders:**
  - Cut 2 **top/bottom outer borders** 3½" x 25".
  - Cut 2 **side outer borders** 3½" x 23½".

- **From assorted cream prints:**
  - Cut 1 **A** 5½" x 23½".
  - Cut 1 **B** 7½" x 9½".
  - Cut 1 **C** 4" x 12".
  - Cut 1 **D** 4" x 14½".
  - Cut 1 **E** 5½" x 8".

- **From gold print for inner borders:**
  - Cut 4 **inner borders** 1¼" x 23½".

- **From assorted blue, red, green, and gold prints:**
  - Cut 4 **corner squares** 3½" x 3½".
  - Cut 1 piece 1¼" x 14½" for **D(a)**.
  - Cut 1 piece 1¼" x 4¾" for **D(b)**.
  - Cut 1 piece 1¼" x 15¼" for **D(c)**.
  - Cut 1 piece 1¼" x 5½" for **D(d)**.
  - Cut a total of 4 **large rectangles** 2½" x 3".
  - Cut a total of 6 **small rectangles** 1½" x 2".

PREPARING THE APPLIQUÉS

*Referring to photo, follow **Preparing Appliqué Pieces**, page 149, and use indicated patterns, pages 99-101, to cut the following pieces from remaining assorted scraps:*

1 **Wall Hanging Alphabet**
3 **Large Hearts**
1 **Hand**
1 **Small Heart**
1 **Flower**
1 **Tag**
5 **Apples**
1 **Equation**
3 **Small Stars**
1 **Large Star**

ASSEMBLING THE WALL HANGING TOP

*Follow **Piecing and Pressing**, page 146, to make wall hanging top.*

1. Referring to photo, use permanent marker to write "For My Teacher" on **Tag**; use dashed lines to write "Teach some Learn some" on **D**.
2. (*Note:* For Steps 2 - 4, refer to **Assembly Diagram**, page 98, for placement.) Assemble 6 **small rectangles** along short sides. Assemble 4 **large rectangles** along long sides. Sew **small**, then **large rectangles** to **B**.
3. Assemble pieces **D** and **D(a) - (d)**, starting with **D(a)** along bottom edge, adding **D(b)** to right edge, then **D(c)** to top and **D(d)** to left edge.
4. Assemble **A**, **B**, **C**, **D**, **E**, and **Schoolhouse Block** to make center section of wall hanging top.
5. Refer to photo and follow **Almost Invisible Appliqué**, page 149, to stitch **appliqué pieces** to center section.
6. Attach **top**, **bottom**, then **side inner borders** to center section.
7. Sew 1 **corner square** to each end of each **side outer border**. Attach **top**, **bottom**, then **side outer borders** to complete **Wall Hanging Top**.

COMPLETING THE WALL HANGING

1. Follow **Quilting**, page 152, to mark, layer, and quilt, using **Quilting Diagram**, page 98, as a suggestion. Our wall hanging is machine quilted.
2. Sew buttons to stars.
3. Follow **Making a Hanging Sleeve**, page 157, to attach hanging sleeve.
4. Follow **Binding**, page 155, to bind wall hanging using 2"w straight-grain binding with overlapped corners. When preparing wall hanging for binding, trim backing and batting even with wall hanging top edges.

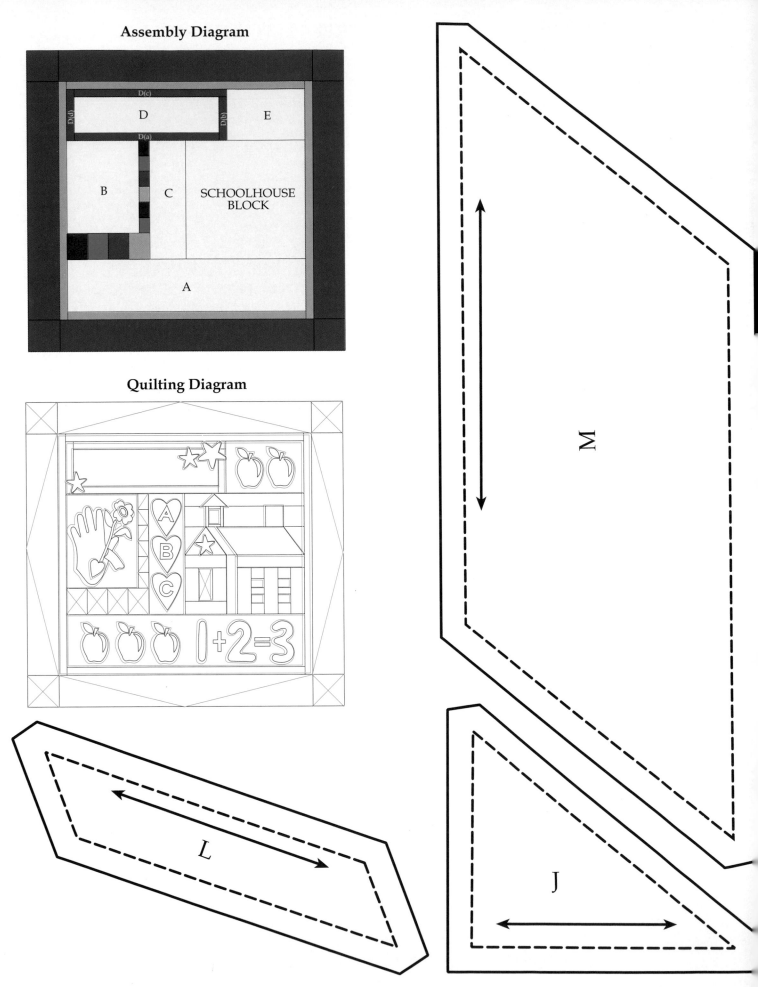

Assembly Diagram

D(c)

D(d)

D

D(b)

E

D(a)

B

C

SCHOOLHOUSE
BLOCK

A

Quilting Diagram

A

B

C

1+2=3

M

L

J

Pillow Alphabet

Apple

K

Large Heart

Small Star

Alphabet

A

B

C

Large Star

Equation

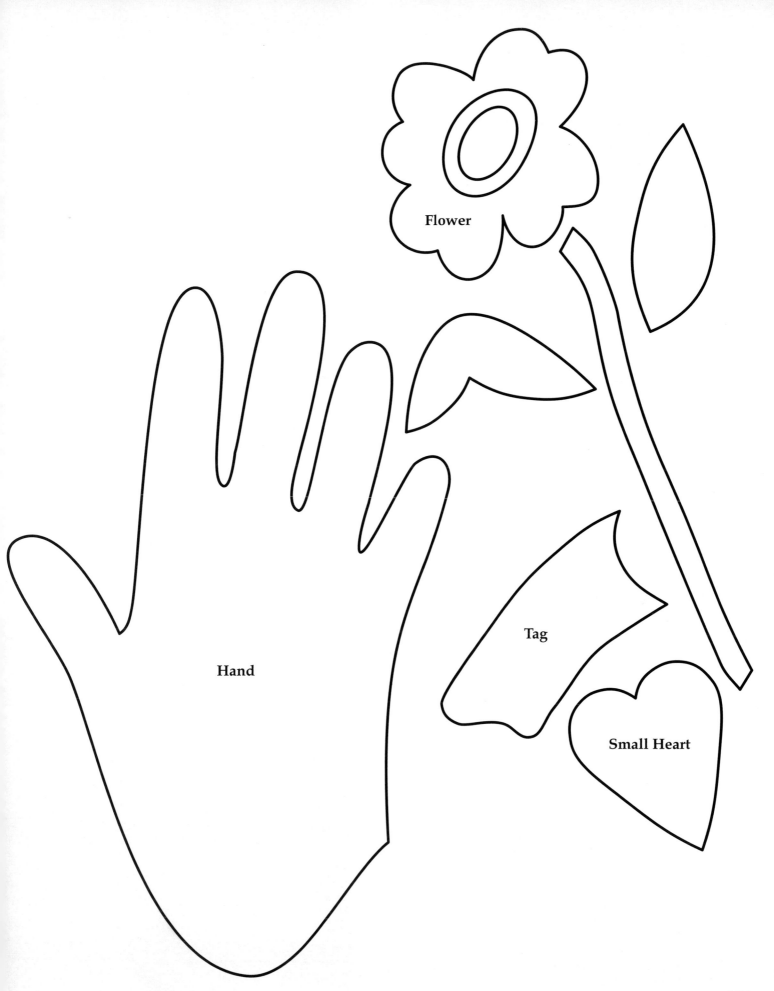

Flower

Hand

Tag

Small Heart

TRIPLE IRISH CHAIN

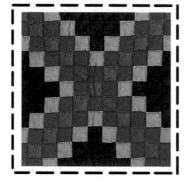

One of the oldest block patterns, the Irish Chain design was developed from a simple shape — the square. Early quilts made with this pattern were tediously crafted using a paper template to cut each patch separately. We've alleviated that tiresome task, however, replacing it with modern rotary-cutting and strip-piecing techniques for our Triple Irish Chain quilt. Pieced in rich solid shades, the style of the quilt is reminiscent of the designs traditionally created by Amish craftswomen of Ohio. The pattern is enhanced with a Seminole patchwork border and intricate flower, feather, and cable quilting.

TRIPLE IRISH CHAIN QUILT

SKILL LEVEL: 1 2 **3** 4 5
BLOCK SIZE: 10½" x 10½"
QUILT SIZE: 89" x 99"

YARDAGE REQUIREMENTS

Yardage is based on 45"w fabric.

 5 yds of navy solid
3¾ yds of purple solid
2⅜ yds of red solid
2⅛ yds of teal solid
8¼ yds for backing
1⅛ yds for binding
120" x 120" batting

CUTTING OUT THE PIECES

All measurements include a ¼" seam allowance. Follow Rotary Cutting, page 144, to cut fabric.

1. **From navy solid:**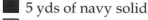
   - Cut 3 selvage-to-selvage strips 8"w. From these strips, cut 15 **squares** 8" x 8".

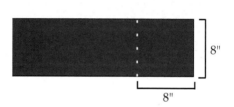

square (cut 15)

8"

8"

   - Cut 16 selvage-to-selvage **strips** 2"w.
   - Cut 4 selvage-to-selvage **strips** 5"w.
   - Cut 2 lengthwise strips 9" x 92" for **top/bottom outer borders**.
   - Cut 2 lengthwise strips 9" x 86" for **side outer borders**.

2. **From purple solid:**
   - Cut 19 selvage-to-selvage **strips** 2"w.
   - Cut 2 lengthwise strips 2" x 83" for **side middle borders**.
   - Cut 2 lengthwise strips 2" x 72" for **top/bottom middle borders**.
   - Cut 2 lengthwise strips 2" x 63½" for **side inner borders**.
   - Cut 2 lengthwise strips 2" x 56" for **top/bottom inner borders**.

3. **From red solid:**
   - Cut 36 selvage-to-selvage **strips** 2"w.

4. **From teal solid:**
   - Cut 32 selvage-to-selvage **strips** 2"w.

ASSEMBLING THE QUILT TOP

Follow Piecing and Pressing, page 146, to make quilt top

1. Assemble 2"w **strips** to make **Strip Set A**. Make 2 **Strip Set A's**. Cut across **Strip Set A's** at 2" intervals to make 30 **Unit 1's**.

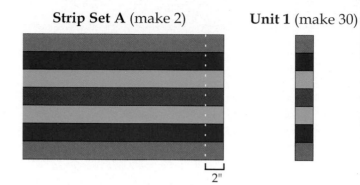

Strip Set A (make 2)   **Unit 1** (make 30)

2"

2. Assemble 2"w **strips** to make **Strip Set B**. Make 2 **Strip Set B's**. Cut across **Strip Set B's** at 2" intervals to make 30 **Unit 2's**.

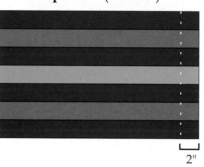

Strip Set B (make 2)   **Unit 2** (make 30)

2"

3. Assemble 2"w **strips** to make **Strip Set C**. Make 2 **Strip Set C's**. Cut across **Strip Set C's** at 2" intervals to make 30 **Unit 3's**.

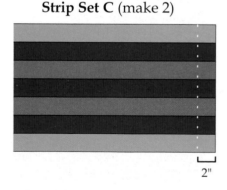

Strip Set C (make 2)   **Unit 3** (make 30)

2"

4. Assemble 2"w **strips** to make 1 **Strip Set D**. Cut across **Strip Set D** at 2" intervals to make 15 **Unit 4's**.

104

Strip Set D (make 1)

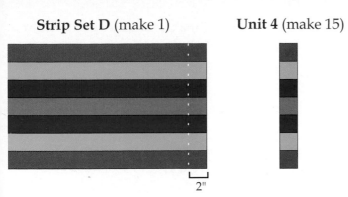

Unit 4 (make 15)

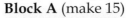

2"

8. Assemble 2 **Unit 1's**, 2 **Unit 2's**, 2 **Unit 3's**, and 1 **Unit 4** to make **Block A**. Make 15 **Block A's**.

Block A (make 15)

5. Assemble 2"w **strips** and 5"w **strip** to make **Strip Set E**. Make 2 **Strip Set E's**. Cut across **Strip Set E's** at 2" intervals to make 30 **Unit 5's**.

Strip Set E (make 2)

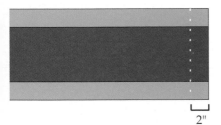

2"

Unit 5 (make 30)

9. Assemble 2 **Unit 5's**, 1 **square**, and 2 **Unit 6's** to make **Block B**. Make 15 **Block B's**.

Block B (make 15)

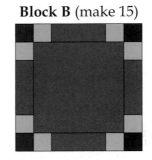

6. Assemble 2"w **strips** and 5"w **strip** to make **Strip Set F**. Make 2 **Strip Set F's**. Cut across **Strip Set F's** at 2" intervals to make 30 **Unit 6's**.

Strip Set F (make 2)

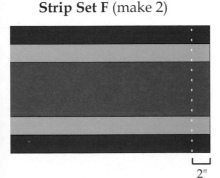

2"

Unit 6 (make 30)

10. Assemble 3 **Block A's** and 2 **Block B's** to make **Row A**. Make 3 **Row A's**.

Row A (make 3)

11. Assemble 3 **Block B's** and 2 **Block A's** to make **Row B**. Make 3 **Row B's**.

Row B (make 3)

7. Assemble 2"w **strips** to make **Strip Set G**. Make 6 **Strip Set G's**. Cut across **Strip Set G's** at 2" intervals to make 126 **Border Units**.

Strip Set G (make 6)   **Border Unit** (make 126)

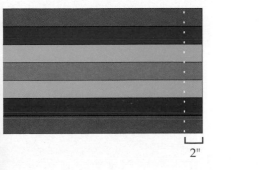

2"

12. Referring to **Quilt Top Diagram**, page 107, assemble **Rows** to make center section of quilt top.
13. Attach **side**, then **top** and **bottom inner borders** to center section of quilt top.

14. Use a seam ripper to take apart 12 **Border Units** to make 24 **Partial Units** as shown.

Partial Units (make 24)

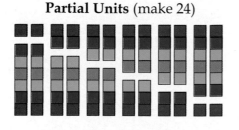

15. To make each **Top/Bottom Seminole Patchwork Border**, assemble 26 **Border Units**, then add 6 **Partial Units** to right end.

Top/Bottom Seminole Patchwork Border (make 2)

16. To make each **Side Seminole Patchwork Border**, assemble 31 **Border Units**, then add 6 **Partial Units** to right end.

Side Seminole Patchwork Border (make 2)

17. Referring to **Fig. 2**, line up ¼" ruler marking (shown in pink) with outermost seam intersections and trim excess fabric from each long edge of each border to complete **Seminole Patchwork Borders**.

Fig. 2

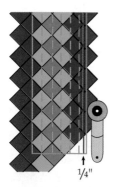

¼"

18. Sew **Seminole Patchwork Borders** to top, bottom, then sides of center section of quilt top, beginning and ending seams exactly ¼" from each corner of quilt top and backstitching at beginning and end of stitching.

19. Fold 1 corner of quilt top diagonally with right sides together, matching outer edges of borders as shown in **Fig. 3**. Beginning at point where previous seams ended, stitch to outer corner. Repeat with remaining corners.

Fig. 3

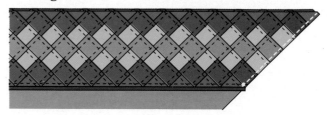

20. Follow **Adding Squared Borders**, page 151, to attach **side**, then **top** and **bottom middle borders**. Attach **side**, then **top** and **bottom outer borders** to complete **Quilt Top**.

COMPLETING THE QUILT

1. Follow **Quilting**, page 152, to mark, layer, and quilt, using **Quilting Diagram** as a suggestion. Our quilt is hand quilted using classic cable, flower, and feather designs.
2. Cut a 34" square of binding fabric. Follow **Binding**, page 155, to bind quilt using 2½"w bias binding with mitered corners.

Quilting Diagram

BLUE
CATHEDRAL

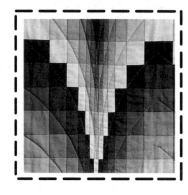

Known *for their fantastic color gradations, bargello designs have been popular for upholstery and needlework since the 17th century. We adapted one of the traditional patterns to quilting for our dramatic Blue Cathedral wall hanging. Its beautiful range of indigos is easy to achieve using a new shaded fabric that re-creates the look of expensive hand-dyed fabric without the high cost. One of our fastest — and easiest — projects, this decorative accent is made with rotary-cut, strip-pieced units that are staggered for the bargello effect. For added flair, we machine quilted the elegant arch design using metallic thread.*

BLUE CATHEDRAL WALL HANGING

SKILL LEVEL: 1 2 3 4 5
WALL HANGING SIZE: 38" x 42"

*Our wall hanging uses **ColorBars**™ fabric, which has seven 6"w lengthwise bands of gradating shades of color. It comes in several color ranges and is available in many quilt and fabric stores.*

YARDAGE REQUIREMENTS

Yardage is based on 45"w fabric.

- 1½ yds of blue ColorBars™
- ¼ yd of dark blue print
- ⅝ yd of blue print
  1½ yds for backing and hanging sleeve
  ½ yd for binding
  41" x 45" batting

CUTTING OUT THE PIECES

*All measurements include a ¼" seam allowance. Follow **Rotary Cutting**, page 144, to cut fabric.*

1. **From blue ColorBars™:**
   - Cut 2 lengthwise strips 2½"w from **each** shade of color to make a total of 14 **strips**.
2. **From dark blue print:**
   - Cut 4 selvage-to-selvage strips 1¼"w for **inner borders**.
3. **From blue print:**
   - Cut 4 selvage-to-selvage strips 4½"w for **outer borders**.

ASSEMBLING THE WALL HANGING TOP

*Follow **Piecing and Pressing**, page 146, to make wall hanging top.*

1. Arranging colors from dark to light and repeating once, assemble ColorBars™ **strips** to make **Unit 1**.

Unit 1

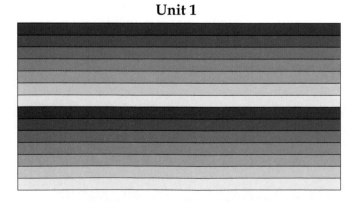

2. With right sides together and matching long raw edges, sew final lengthwise seam of **Unit 1** to form a tube (**Fig. 1**).

Fig. 1

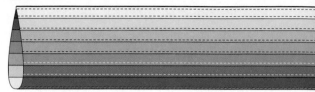

3. Referring to **Fig. 2**, cut the following circular strips:
   - Cut 2 **A's** 4¾"w.
   - Cut 3 **B's** 3"w.
   - Cut 4 **C's** 2"w.
   - Cut 4 **D's** 1½"w.
   - Cut 4 **E's** 1⅛"w.
   - Cut 10 **F's** ⅞"w.

Fig. 2

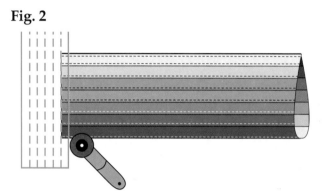

4. Working from left to right, lay out the circular strips in the following sequence:
   A-B-C-D-E-F-F-F-F-F-E-D-C-B-C-D-E-F-F-F-F-F-E-D-C-B-A
5. Refer to **Wall Hanging Top Diagram** to determine which color should be at the top of each vertical strip in the wall hanging top. Use a seam ripper to remove the seam above the determined top square in each circular strip (**Fig. 3**).

Fig. 3

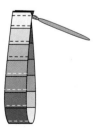

6. Referring to **Wall Hanging Top Diagram**, assemble strips in determined sequence to complete center section of wall hanging top.

7. Follow **Adding Squared Borders**, page 151, to add **side**, then **top** and **bottom inner borders** to center section of wall hanging top. Add **side**, then **top** and **bottom outer borders** to complete **Wall Hanging Top**.

COMPLETING THE WALL HANGING

1. Follow **Quilting**, page 152, to mark, layer, and quilt, using **Quilting Diagram** as a suggestion. Our wall hanging is machine quilted using silver metallic thread.
2. Follow **Making a Hanging Sleeve**, page 157, to attach a hanging sleeve to wall hanging.
3. Follow **Binding**, page 155, to bind wall hanging with 2¹/₂"w straight-grain binding with overlapped corners.

Quilting Diagram

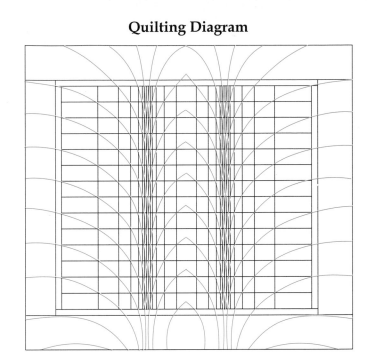

Wall Hanging Top Diagram

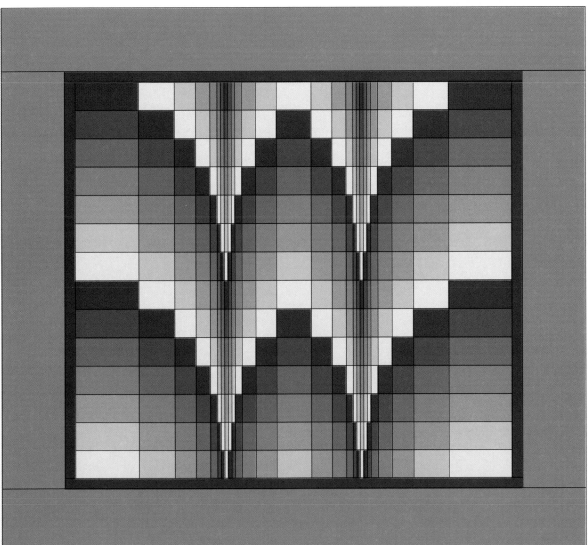

ADIRONDACK COLLECTION

Far upstate from the bustle of New York City lie the secluded, peaceful peaks of the Adirondack Mountains. Known for pristine lakes and spectacular winters, the region has long been a popular retreat where simple pleasures are the greatest rewards. Our Adirondack Collection captures that spirit with an array of rustic designs. A handsome accent for the lodge, our Adirondack quilt is a variation of the Bear's Paw pattern. A variety of fabrics is used to create its complex-looking arrangement, but the pattern is actually a breeze to make using our grid-piecing method for the triangle-squares. The woodsy motifs featured on the pillow flip are quickly fused in place and machine appliquéd using clear nylon thread.

Our embellished winter accessories (left) will keep you stylishly warm. Simple motifs are fused to purchased scarves, mittens, and gloves and edged with blanket stitching. For evenings by the fire, you'll love this comfy floor pillow (below), which features our Bear's Paw design. Spruce up a bare wall with our bear wall hanging (opposite)! It features pieced blocks and machine appliqués.

*W*hat could be more perfect for chilly fall outings than our woodland sweaters for him and her! For our grizzly bear wear, we simply pieced the block, fused on the appliqué, and sewed it all in place using easy blanket stitching. The grove of designs on our evergreen sweater is even easier to assemble — just fuse the motifs on and add blanket stitching.

ADIRONDACK QUILT

SKILL LEVEL: 1 2 3 4 5
BLOCK SIZE: 12 1/4" x 12 1/4"
QUILT SIZE: 82" x 108"

YARDAGE REQUIREMENTS

Yardage is based on 45"w fabric.

- 4 1/4 yds of dark brown check
- 3 1/2 yds of tan print
- 2 3/4 yds **total** of assorted plaids, stripes, and checks (our quilt uses 5 different fabrics)
- 2 3/8 yds of red print
- 1 1/4 yds of dark red print
- 7/8 yd of green solid
- 3/8 yd of gold plaid
- 1 fat quarter (18" x 22" piece) **each** of green plaid and green print for tree appliqués
- 7 3/4 yds for backing
- 1 yd for binding
- 120" x 120" batting

You will also need:

paper-backed fusible web
transparent monofilament thread for appliqué

CUTTING OUT THE PIECES

*All measurements include a 1/4" seam allowance. Follow **Rotary Cutting**, page 144, to cut fabric.*

1. **From dark brown check:**
   - Cut 6 selvage-to-selvage **strips** 5 3/4"w.
   - Cut 2 lengthwise strips 4" x 104" for **side outer borders**.
   - Cut 2 lengthwise strips 4" x 85" for **top/bottom outer borders**.
   - Cut 21 strips 2 1/4"w from fabric width remaining after cutting borders. From these strips, cut a total of 84 **rectangles** 2 1/4" x 5 3/4".
2. **From tan print:**
   - Cut 1 lengthwise strip 13 3/4" x 76" for **pillow flip**.
   - Cut 8 **large rectangles** 17" x 20" for triangle-squares.
3. **From assorted plaids, stripes, and checks:**
   - Cut 21 selvage-to-selvage strips 4"w. From these strips, cut 168 **large squares** 4" x 4". (For each of the 42 blocks, you will need 4 matching **large squares**.)
4. **From red print:**
   - Cut 1 lengthwise strip 1 1/4" x 76" for **top inner border**.
   - Cut 4 **large rectangles** 17" x 20" for triangle-squares.
5. **From dark red print:**
   - Cut 4 **large rectangles** 17" x 20" for triangle-squares.
6. **From green solid:**
   - Cut 10 selvage-to-selvage strips 2 1/4"w. From these strips, cut 168 **squares** 2 1/4" x 2 1/4".
7. **From gold plaid:**
   - Cut 3 selvage-to-selvage **strips** 2 1/4"w.

PREPARING THE APPLIQUÉS

*Follow **Preparing Appliqué Pieces**, page 149, to cut pieces using patterns, pages 125-127.*

1. **From dark brown check:**
   - Cut 4 **Bears** (2 in reverse).
2. **From dark red print:**
   - Cut 5 **Small Tree Trunks**.
   - Cut 3 **Large Tree Trunks**.
3. **From green solid:**
   - Cut 2 **Tree A's**.
4. **From gold plaid:**
   - Cut 3 **Large Moons**.
5. **From green plaid:**
   - Cut 3 **Tree A's**.
6. **From green print:**
   - Cut 3 **Tree A's**.

ASSEMBLING THE QUILT TOP

*Follow **Piecing and Pressing**, page 146, to make quilt top.*

1. Assemble **strips** as shown to make **Strip Set**. Make 3 **Strip Sets**. Cut across **Strip Sets** at 2 1/4" intervals to make 42 **Unit 1's**.

Strip Set (make 3) **Unit 1** (make 42)

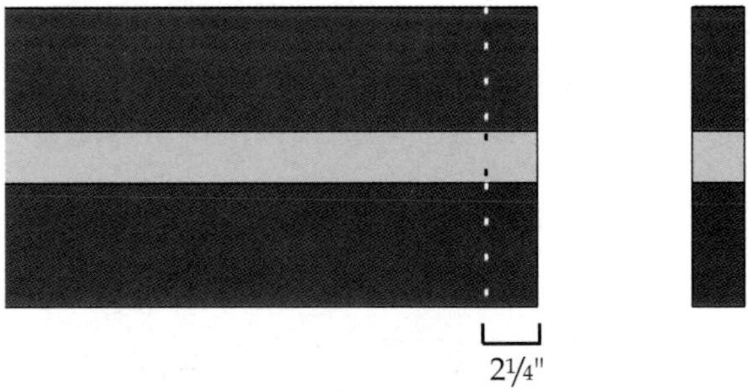

2. To make triangle-square A's, place 1 tan print and 1 red print **large rectangle** right sides together. Referring to **Fig. 1**, page 118, follow Steps 1 - 3 of **Making Triangle-Squares**, page 147, to draw a grid of 42 squares 2 5/8" x 2 5/8". Referring to **Fig. 2**, page 118, for stitching direction, follow Steps 4 - 6 of **Making Triangle-Squares** to make 84 **triangle-square A's**. Repeat to complete 336 **triangle-square A's**.

Fig. 1

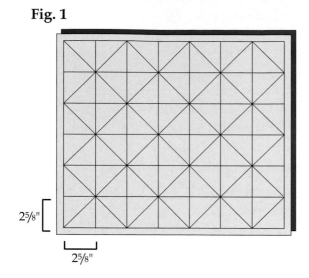

 2⅝"

2⅝"

Fig. 2

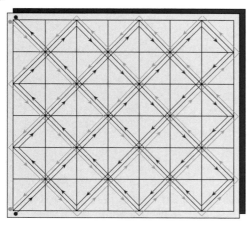

triangle-square A (make 336)

3. Using dark red print **large rectangles** and remaining tan print **large rectangles**, repeat Step 2 to make a total of 336 **triangle-square B's**.

triangle-square B (make 336)

4. Assemble 2 **triangle-square A's** to make **Unit 2**. Make 84 **Unit 2's**.

Unit 2 (make 84)

5. Assemble 2 **triangle-square A's** and 1 **square** to make **Unit 3**. Make 84 **Unit 3's**.

Unit 3 (make 84)

6. Assemble 1 **Unit 2**, 1 **large square**, and 1 **Unit 3** to make **Unit 4**. Make 84 **Unit 4's**.

Unit 4 (make 84)

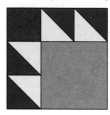

7. Assemble 2 **Unit 4's** and 1 **rectangle** to make **Unit 5**. Make 42 **Unit 5's**.

Unit 5 (make 42)

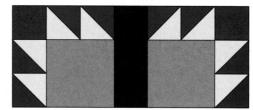
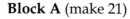

8. Assemble 1 **Unit 1** and 2 **Unit 5's** to make **Block A**. Make 21 **Block A's**.

Block A (make 21)

9. Use **triangle-square B's** and repeat Steps 4 - 8 to make 21 **Block B's**.

Block B (make 21)

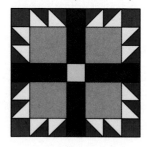

10. Referring to **Quilt Top Diagram**, page 120, assemble **Blocks** into rows; sew rows together to make center section of quilt top.
11. Referring to **Quilt Top Diagram**, follow **Almost Invisible Appliqué**, page 149, to stitch appliqués to **pillow flip**.
12. Follow **Adding Squared Borders**, page 151, to attach **pillow flip**, then **top inner border** to center section of quilt top.
13. Follow **Adding Squared Borders**, page 151, to attach **side**, then **top** and **bottom outer borders** to complete **Quilt Top**.

COMPLETING THE QUILT
1. Follow **Quilting**, page 152, to mark, layer, and quilt, using **Quilting Diagram** as a suggestion. Our quilt is hand quilted.
2. Cut a 34" square of binding fabric. Follow **Binding**, page 155, to bind quilt using $2^{1}/_{2}$"w bias binding with mitered corners.

Quilting Diagram

ADIRONDACK WALL HANGING

SKILL LEVEL: 1 2 3 4 5
BLOCK SIZE: 12¼" x 12¼"
WALL HANGING SIZE: 32" x 32"

YARDAGE REQUIREMENTS
Yardage is based on 45"w fabric.

- ⅝ yd **each** of dark brown check and light brown plaid
- ¼ yd **each** of green stripe, plaid, and solid
- 1 fat quarter (18" x 22" piece) **each** of tan print and red print
- scraps of gold plaid, green print, and dark red print
- 1 yd for backing
- ½ yd for binding
- 36" x 36" batting
- paper-backed fusible web
- transparent monofilament thread for appliqué

CUTTING OUT THE PIECES
All measurements include a ¼" seam allowance. Follow Rotary Cutting, page 144, to cut fabric.

1. **From dark brown check:**
   - Cut 4 strips 4" x 25" for **borders**.

2. **From light brown plaid:**
   - Cut 1 selvage-to-selvage strip 4"w. From this strip, cut 8 **small squares** 4" x 4".
   - Cut 1 selvage-to-selvage strip 11"w. From this strip, cut 2 **large squares** 11" x 11".

3. **From green stripe:**
   - Cut 2 selvage-to-selvage strips 2¼"w. From these strips, cut 8 **rectangles** 2¼" x 5¾".

4. **From green plaid:**
   - Cut 4 squares 4" x 4" for **border squares**.

5. **From green solid:**
   - Cut 1 selvage-to-selvage strip 2¼"w. From this strip, cut 10 **squares** 2¼" x 2¼".

6. **From tan print:**
   - Cut 1 **large rectangle** 12" x 20" for triangle-squares.

7. **From red print:**
   - Cut 1 **large rectangle** 12" x 20" for triangle-squares.

8. **From gold plaid:**
   - Cut 2 squares 2¼" x 2¼".

PREPARING THE APPLIQUÉS
Follow Preparing Appliqué Pieces, page 149, to cut pieces using patterns, pages 125 - 127.

1. **From dark brown check:**
   - Cut 1 **Bear**.

2. **From green plaid:**
   - Cut 2 **Tree A's**.

3. **From gold plaid:**
   - Cut 2 **Large Moons**.

4. **From green print:**
   - Cut 1 **Tree A**.

5. **From dark red print:** ■
   - Cut 1 **Small Tree Trunk**.
   - Cut 1 **Large Tree Trunk**.

ASSEMBLING THE WALL HANGING TOP
Follow Piecing And Pressing, page 146, to make wall hanging top.

1. Assemble 2 **rectangles** and 1 **square** to make **Unit 1**. Make 2 **Unit 1's**.

Unit 1 (make 2)

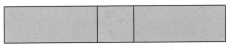

2. To make triangle-squares, place 1 tan print and 1 red print **large rectangle** right sides together. Referring to **Fig. 1**, follow Steps 1 - 3 of **Making Triangle-Squares**, page 147, to draw a grid of 28 squares 2⅝" x 2⅝". Referring to **Fig. 2** for stitching direction, follow Steps 4 - 6 of **Making Triangle-Squares** to make a total of 56 **triangle-squares**.

Fig. 1

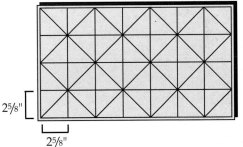

2⅝"

2⅝"

Fig. 2

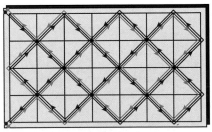

triangle-square (make 56)

3. Follow Steps 4 - 8 of **Assembling the Quilt Top** for **Adirondack Quilt**, page 118, to make 2 **Block A's**. (You will need 2 **Unit 1's**, 8 **Unit 2's**, 8 **Unit 3's**, and 4 **Unit 5's** to complete Block A's.)
4. Assemble 6 **triangle-squares** to make **Unit 6**. Make 2 **Unit 6's**. Assemble 6 **triangle-squares** and 1 **square** to make **Unit 7**. Make 2 **Unit 7's**.

Unit 6 (make 2)

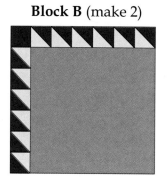

Unit 7 (make 2)

5. Assemble 1 **Unit 6**, 1 **Unit 7**, and 1 **large square** to make **Block B**. Make 2 **Block B's**.

Block B (make 2)

6. Referring to **Wall Hanging Top Diagram**, follow **Almost Invisible Appliqué**, page 149, to stitch appliqués to **Block B's**.
7. Referring to **Wall Hanging Top Diagram**, assemble **Block A's** and **Block B's** to make center section of wall hanging top.
8. Sew 2 **borders** to top and bottom of center section of wall hanging top.
9. Sew 1 **border square** to each end of remaining **borders**. Sew **borders** to sides of center section to complete **Wall Hanging Top**.

COMPLETING THE WALL HANGING

1. Follow **Quilting**, page 152, to mark, layer, and quilt, using **Quilting Diagram** as a suggestion. Our wall hanging is hand quilted.
2. Trim backing and batting even with edges of wall hanging top.
3. Follow **Making a Hanging Sleeve**, page 157, to attach hanging sleeve to wall hanging.
4. Cut an 18" square of binding fabric. Follow **Binding**, page 155, to bind wall hanging using 2"w bias binding with mitered corners.

Wall Hanging Top Diagram

Quilting Diagram

COZY FLOOR PILLOW

BLOCK SIZE: 12$\frac{1}{4}$" x 12$\frac{1}{4}$"
PILLOW SIZE: 29" x 29"

YARDAGE REQUIREMENTS

Yardage is based on 45"w fabric.

- ⬛ $\frac{5}{8}$ yd of dark brown check
- ⬜ $\frac{1}{2}$ yd of tan print
- ⬛ $\frac{1}{8}$ yd of green solid
- ⬛ 1 fat quarter (18" x 22" piece) **each** of red print and dark red print
- ⬛ 1 fat quarter (18" x 22" piece) **each** of 4 different plaids, stripes, and/or checks
- ⬜ 6" x 13" piece of gold plaid
- 1 yd for pillow top backing
- 1 yd for pillow back
- 3$\frac{1}{2}$ yds of 2$\frac{3}{8}$"w bias strip for welting
- 3$\frac{3}{4}$ yds of $\frac{3}{8}$" cord for welting
- 32" x 32" batting
- 28" x 28" pillow form

CUTTING OUT THE PIECES

All measurements include a $\frac{1}{4}$" seam allowance. Follow Rotary Cutting, page 144, to cut fabric.

1. **From dark brown check:** ⬛
   - Cut 2 selvage-to-selvage strips 2$\frac{1}{4}$"w. From these strips, cut 8 **rectangles** 2$\frac{1}{4}$" x 5$\frac{3}{4}$".
   - Cut 2 **strips** 5$\frac{3}{4}$" x 12".
   - Cut 2 strips 2$\frac{1}{2}$" x 28$\frac{1}{2}$" for **top/bottom borders**.
   - Cut 2 strips 2$\frac{1}{2}$" x 25" for **side borders**.

2. **From tan print:** ⬜
   - Cut 2 **squares** 12" x 12" for triangle-squares.

3. **From green solid:** ⬛
   - Cut 1 selvage-to-selvage strip 2$\frac{1}{4}$"w. From this strip, cut 16 **squares** 2$\frac{1}{4}$" x 2$\frac{1}{4}$".

4. **From red print:** ⬛
   - Cut 1 **square** 12" x 12" for triangle-squares.

5. **From dark red print:** ⬛
   - Cut 1 **square** 12" x 12" for triangle-squares.

6. **From *each* plaid, stripe, and/or check:** ⬛
   - Cut 4 **squares** 4" x 4".

7. **From gold plaid:** ⬜
   - Cut 1 **strip** 2$\frac{1}{4}$" x 12".

ASSEMBLING THE PILLOW TOP

Follow Piecing And Pressing, page 146, to make pillow top.

1. Using 12"l **strips**, follow Step 1 of **Assembling the Quilt Top** for **Adirondack Quilt**, page 117, to make 4 **Unit 1's**.

2. To make triangle-square A's, place 1 tan print and 1 red print **square** right sides together. Referring to **Fig. 1**, follow Steps 1 - 3 of **Making Triangle-Squares**, page 147, to draw a grid of 16 squares 2$\frac{5}{8}$" x 2$\frac{5}{8}$". Referring to **Fig. 2** for stitching direction, follow Steps 4 - 6 of **Making Triangle-Squares** to complete 32 **triangle-square A's**.

Fig. 1

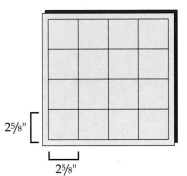

2$\frac{5}{8}$"

2$\frac{5}{8}$"

Fig. 2

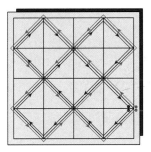

triangle-square A (make 32)

3. Using remaining tan print and dark red print **squares**, repeat Step 2 to make 32 **triangle-square B's**.

triangle-square B (make 32)

4. Follow Steps 4 - 8 of **Assembling the Quilt Top** for **Adirondack Quilt**, page 118, to make 2 **Block A's**. (You will need 2 **Unit 1's**, 8 **Unit 2's**, 8 **Unit 3's**, and 4 **Unit 5's** to complete Block A's.)

5. Use **triangle-square B's** and follow Steps 4 - 8 of **Assembling the Quilt Top** for **Adirondack Quilt**, page 118, to make 2 **Block B's**. (You will need 2 **Unit 1's**, 8 **Unit 2's**, 8 **Unit 3's**, and 4 **Unit 5's** to complete Block B's.)

6. Referring to **Pillow Top Diagram**, assemble **Block A's** and **Block B's** to complete center section of pillow top.
7. Attach **side**, then **top** and **bottom borders** to complete **Pillow Top**.

COMPLETING THE PILLOW
1. Follow **Quilting**, page 152, to mark, layer, and quilt, using **Quilting Diagram**, page 119, as a suggestion. Our pillow top is hand quilted.
2. Follow **Pillow Finishing**, page 158, to complete pillow with welting.

Pillow Top Diagram

GRIZZLY BEAR SWEATER

SUPPLIES
1 sweater
10" x 10" square **each** of dark red print, light brown plaid, and green print
1½ yds of 1½"w bias strip for binding
paper-backed fusible web
embroidery floss

MAKING THE SWEATER
1. Cut 1 square 8⅞" x 8⅞" from dark red print. Cut square once diagonally to make 2 triangles. Repeat to cut 2 green print triangles.
2. Follow **Piecing and Pressing**, page 146, to assemble 1 dark red print and 1 green print triangle to make 1 **square**. (Remaining triangles will not be used.)

3. For binding, press bias strip in half lengthwise with wrong sides together and follow Steps 1 - 7 of **Attaching Binding with Mitered Corners**, page 156, to attach binding to square. Press binding out. Do not fold over to back of square.
4. Use **Bear** pattern, page 126, and follow **Preparing Appliqué Pieces**, page 149, to cut 1 bear from light brown plaid.
5. Referring to photo, fuse bear to square. Use 2 strands of floss to work **Blanket Stitch**, page 158, around edges of bear.
6. Baste square to sweater front.
7. Use 3 strands of floss to work **Blanket Stitch**, page 158, around edges of square. Remove basting stitches.

EVERGREEN SWEATER

SUPPLIES
1 sweater
assorted scraps for appliqués
paper-backed fusible web
embroidery floss

MAKING THE SWEATER
1. Use **Tree A**, **Tree B**, **Tree C**, **Large Moon**, **Small Tree Trunk**, **Medium Tree Trunk**, and **Large Tree Trunk** patterns, pages 125 and 127, and follow **Preparing Appliqué Pieces**, page 149, to cut 1 appliqué from each pattern.
2. Referring to photo, fuse appliqués to sweater.
3. Use 2 strands of floss to work **Blanket Stitch**, page 158, around edges of appliqués.

WINTER CHILL STOPPERS

SUPPLIES
scarf, gloves, and/or mittens
assorted scraps for appliqués
paper-backed fusible web
embroidery floss

MAKING THE CHILL STOPPERS
1. Referring to photo, use desired patterns, pages 125 and 127, and follow **Preparing Appliqué Pieces**, page 149, to cut appliqués from scraps.
2. Referring to photo, fuse appliqués to scarf, gloves, or mittens.
3. Use 2 strands of floss to work **Blanket Stitch**, page 158, around edges of appliqués.

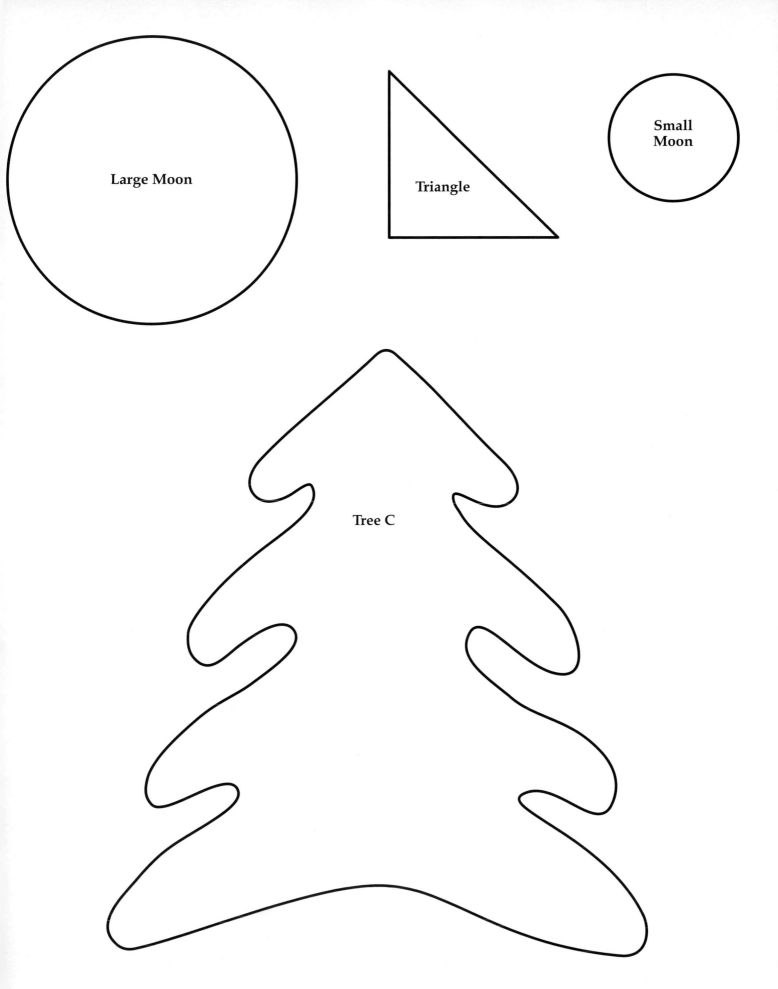

Large Moon

Triangle

Small
Moon

Tree C

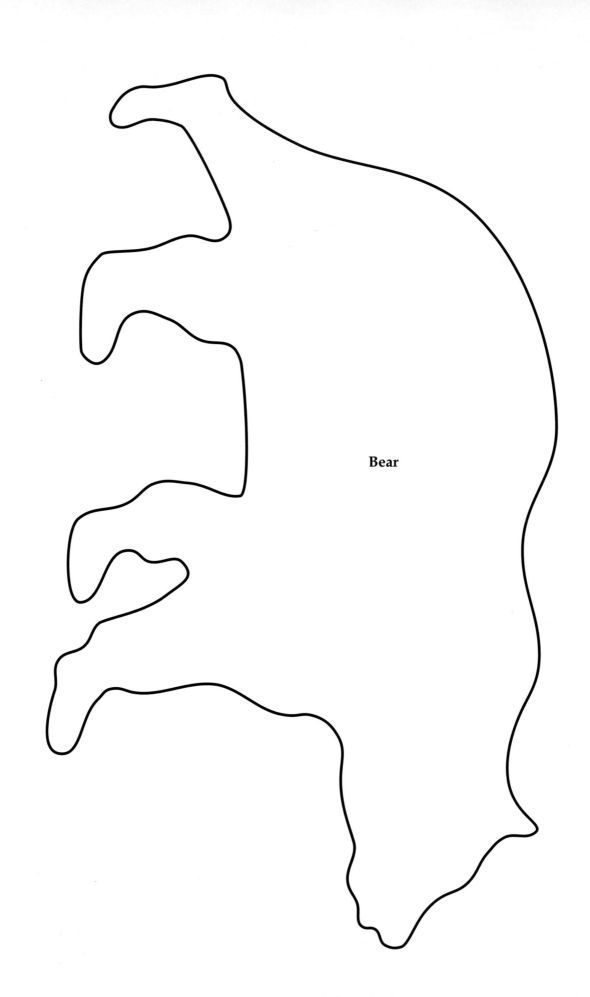

Bear

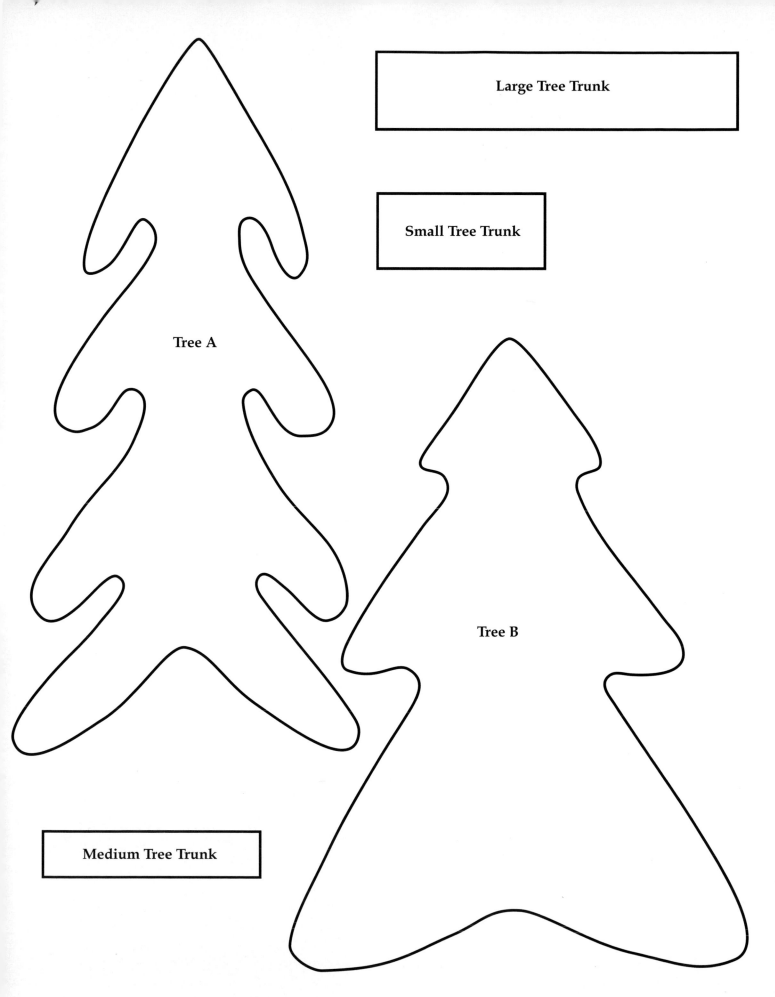

Large Tree Trunk

Small Tree Trunk

Tree A

Tree B

Medium Tree Trunk

127

NINE-PATCH CHAIN

Look closely at this charming quilt and you'll notice that its dainty grid is actually formed with tiny nine-patch blocks. Used as one of the first quilting lessons for many pioneer girls, the nine-patch pattern is perfect for today's beginning quilters as well. Our Nine-Patch Chain is simple to re-create by assembling the strip-pieced blocks and solid squares into long rows. Then the rows are stitched together and finished off with a squared border and basic grid quilting. For a bit of quaint interest, a "humility block" (as seen in the lower left corner of our quilt) can be blended into the design by reversing the colors in one nine patch. Many quilters of old believed that such intentional "errors" ensured good luck.

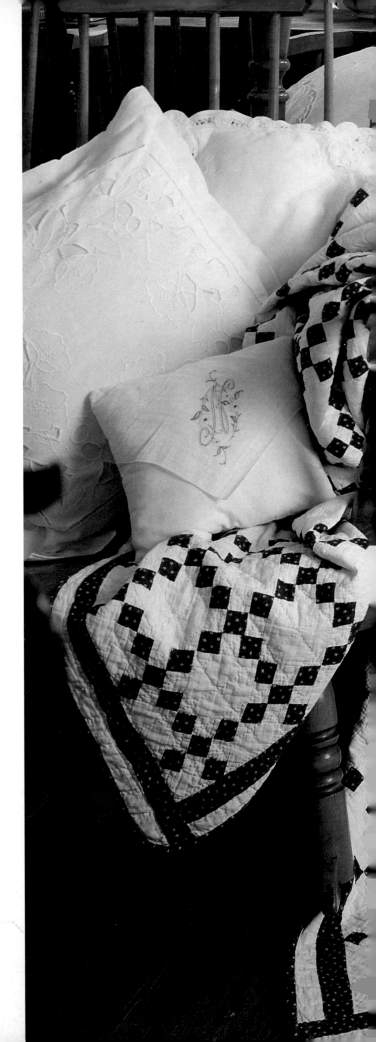

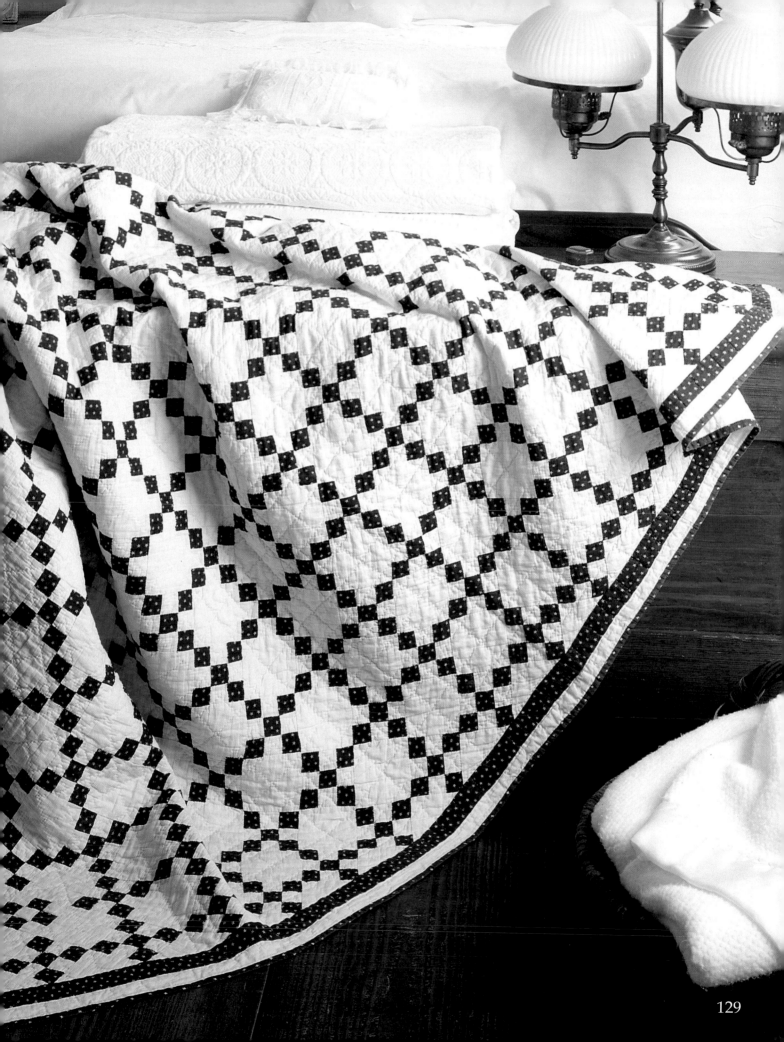

NINE-PATCH CHAIN QUILT

SKILL LEVEL: 1 2 3 4 5
BLOCK SIZE: 2⅝" x 2⅝"
QUILT SIZE: 76" x 76"

YARDAGE REQUIREMENTS

Yardage is based on 45"w fabric.

 3 yds of blue print

5 yds of white solid
4¾ yds for backing
⅞ yd for binding
81" x 96" batting

CUTTING OUT THE PIECES

All measurements include a ¼" seam allowance. Follow
Rotary Cutting, page 144, to cut fabric.

1. **From blue print:**
   - Cut 13 selvage-to-selvage **strips** 1⅜"w.
   - Cut 2 lengthwise strips 1½" x 79" for **top/bottom inner borders**.
   - Cut 2 lengthwise strips 1½" x 75" for **side inner borders**.
   - From remaining fabric, cut 57 additional **strips** 1⅜"w.

2. **From white solid:**
   - Cut 25 selvage-to-selvage strips 3⅛"w. From these strips, cut 324 **setting squares** 3⅛" x 3⅛".

setting square (cut 324)

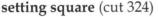
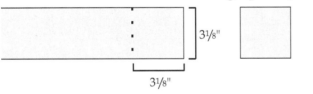

   - Cut 3 selvage-to-selvage strips 5"w. From these strips, cut 18 squares 5" x 5". Cut squares twice diagonally to make 72 **side setting triangles**.

square (cut 18)   **side setting triangle** (cut 72)

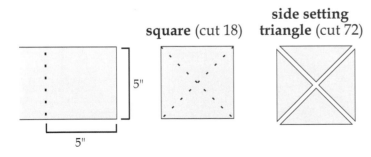

   - Cut 2 lengthwise strips 1½" x 79" for **top/bottom outer borders**.
   - Cut 2 lengthwise strips 1½" x 75" for **side outer borders**.
   - Cut 56 **strips** 1⅜"w from remaining fabric width.

130

   - Cut 2 squares 2¾" x 2¾". Cut squares once diagonally to make 4 **corner setting triangles**.

square (cut 2)   **corner setting triangle** (cut 4)

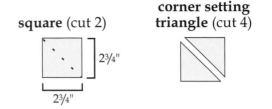

ASSEMBLING THE QUILT TOP

Follow Piecing and Pressing, page 146, to make quilt top.

1. Assemble **strips** (of the same length) to make **Strip Set A**. Make 28 **Strip Set A's**. Cut across **Strip Set A's** at 1⅜" intervals to make 722 **Unit 1's**.

Strip Set A (make 28)   **Unit 1** (make 722)

2. Assemble **strips** (some blue strips are longer than white strips) to make **Strip Set B**. Make 14 **Strip Set B's**. Cut across **Strip Set B's** at 1⅜" intervals to make 361 **Unit 2's**.

Strip Set B (make 14)   **Unit 2** (make 361)

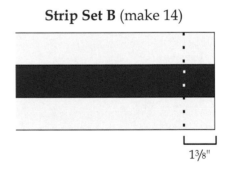

3. Assemble 2 **Unit 1's** and 1 **Unit 2** to make **Block**. Make 361 **Blocks**.

Block (make 361)

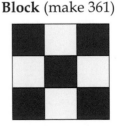

4. Refer to **Assembly Diagram** to assemble **corner setting triangles**, **Blocks**, **setting triangles**, and **setting squares** into diagonal rows; sew rows together to complete center section of quilt top.

5. Assemble **borders** to make **Border Unit**. Make 2 **Side Border Units** and 2 **Top/Bottom Border Units**.

Border Unit

6. Referring to **Quilt Top Diagram**, page 132, follow **Adding Squared Borders**, page 151, to attach **Side**, then **Top** and **Bottom Border Units** to center section to complete **Quilt Top**. Round off corners as shown.

COMPLETING THE QUILT

1. Follow **Quilting**, page 152, to mark, layer, and quilt, using **Quilting Diagram**, page 133, as a suggestion. Our quilt is hand quilted.

2. Cut a 30" square of binding fabric. Follow **Binding**, page 155, to make 2½"w bias binding. To attach binding, follow Steps 1 and 2 of **Attaching Binding with Mitered Corners**, page 156, to pin binding to front of quilt. Easing binding around curves, sew binding to quilt. Fold binding over to quilt backing; blindstitch in place.

Assembly Diagram

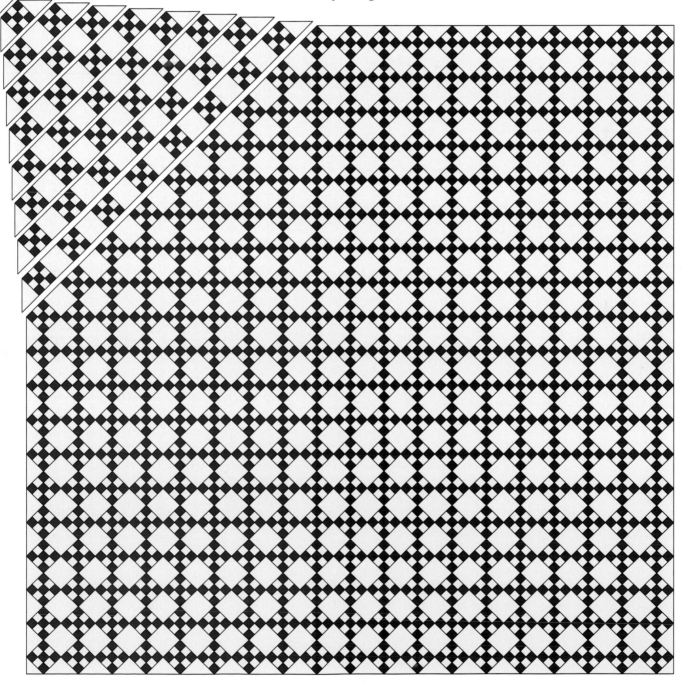

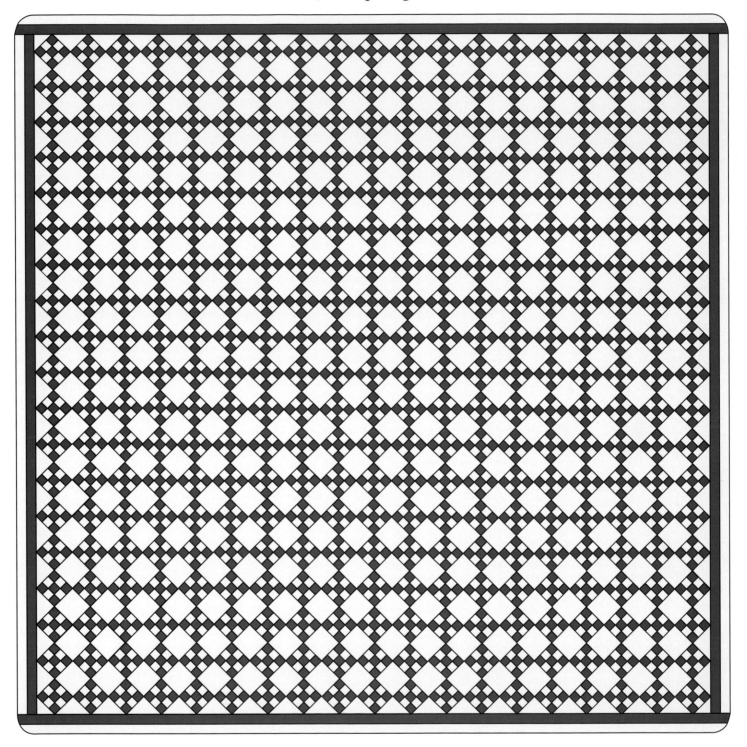

Quilting Diagram

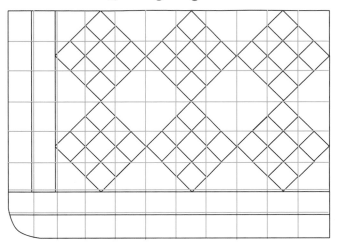

┏ ━ ━ ━ ━ ━ ━ ━ ━ ━ ━ ━ ━ ━ ━ ━ ━ **QUICK TIP** ━ ━ ━ ━ ━ ━ ━ ━ ━ ┓

SELECTING THE RIGHT BATTING

Choosing the right batting will make your quilting job easier. Battings come in many different fibers and densities and give your quilt its personality and warmth.

- ***Bonded polyester batting*** *is treated with a protective coating to stabilize the fibers and reduce "bearding," a process where bits of batting fibers work their way up through the quilt fabrics. It launders well with minimal to no shrinkage. Quilting at least every 3" to 4" is recommended.*

  *Choose **low-loft batting** for fine hand and machine quilting. It is lightweight, easy to quilt, and will give your completed project the "flat" appearance of a traditional quilt.*

  *Select **extra-loft**, **high-loft**, or **fat batting** when tying a quilt to give your project the puffy look of a comforter. Although these thicker battings can be hand quilted, you may not be satisfied with the end result.*

- ***Cotton/Polyester batting*** *may be machine or hand quilted. This batting must be quilted at least every 3" to 4". It may not shrink as much as 100% cotton batting, but some shrinkage is still a possibility.*

- ***Cotton batting*** *may be machine or hand quilted, but must be quilted more closely than bonded or cotton/polyester battings for durability and to prevent shifting. Because of shrinkage that occurs during laundering, cotton batting gives your quilt the flat, wrinkled appearance similar to that of antique quilts. In fact, some manufacturers suggest prewashing the batting to help minimize shrinkage.*

- ***Wool and Silk batting*** *are not as popular and are generally more expensive. Bearding is a possibility with wool. There are also particular laundering specifications for each type of batting. Follow the manufacturer's instructions carefully if you decide to try one of these.*

AUTUMN BASKETS

Since the late 1700's, quilters have treasured basket motifs, often pairing them with flowers, fruit, and a bounty of favorite things. The versatile designs symbolized the promise of abundant harvests and beautiful blossoms to come. For our Autumn Baskets quilt, we chose the rustic hues of the gathering season and a medallion-style arrangement for the pieced and appliquéd blocks. The baskets are fast to assemble using our easy grid-piecing technique. Securing the appliqués is simplified by using paper-backed fusible web and clear monofilament thread.

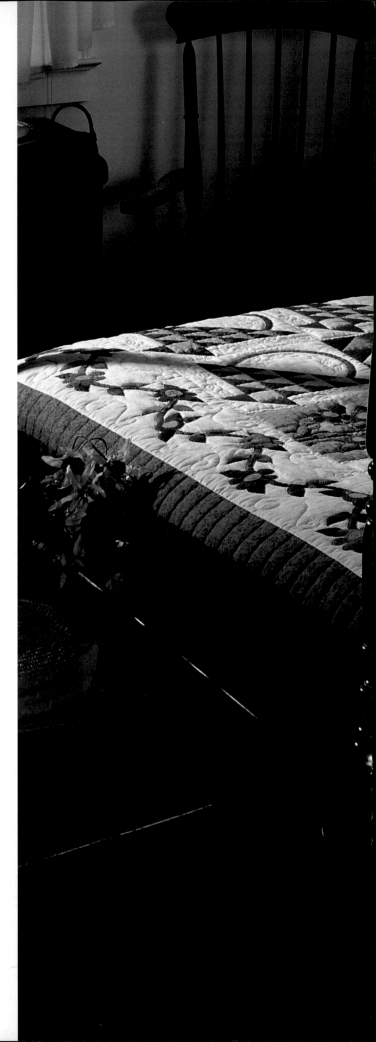

AUTUMN BASKETS QUILT

SKILL LEVEL: 1 2 3 4 5
BLOCK SIZE: 12" x 12"
QUILT SIZE: 86" x 102"

YARDAGE REQUIREMENTS
Yardage is based on 45"w fabric.

- 2⅞ yds of dark cream solid
- 2¾ yds of brown print for outer borders
- 2½ yds of dark gold print for inner borders
- 1 yd of green plaid for vines
- ⅞ yd of tan print for appliquéd block background
- ⅜ yd **each** of 9 light tan prints
- ⅜ yd **each** of 16 assorted brown, gold, green, and rust prints and/or plaids
- ¼ yd of gold print for medallion borders
- 7⅞ yds for backing
- 1 yd for binding
- 120" x 120" batting

You will also need:
- paper-backed fusible web
- transparent monofilament thread for appliqué
- ½" bias pressing bar

CUTTING OUT THE PIECES
All measurements include a ¼" seam allowance. Follow Rotary Cutting, page 144, to cut fabric unless otherwise indicated.

1. **From dark cream solid:**
   - Cut 3 selvage-to-selvage strips 10⅞"w. From these strips, cut 8 squares 10⅞" x 10⅞". Cut squares once diagonally to make 16 **large triangles**.
   - Cut 2 lengthwise strips 8½" x 60½" for **border panels**.
   - From remainder, cut 32 **rectangles** 2½" x 8½" and 8 squares 4⅞" x 4⅞". Cut squares once diagonally to make 16 **medium triangles**.

2. **From brown print for outer borders:**
   - Cut 2 lengthwise strips 10½" x 89½" for **top/bottom outer borders**.
   - Cut 2 lengthwise strips 10½" x 85½" for **side outer borders**.

3. **From dark gold print for inner borders:**
   - Cut 2 lengthwise strips 3¼" x 80" for **side inner borders**.
   - Cut 2 lengthwise strips 3¼" x 69½" for **top/bottom inner borders**.

4. **From green plaid for vine:**
   - Cut 4 **bias strips** 1½" x 36".

5. **From tan print for appliquéd block background:**
   - Cut 2 selvage-to-selvage strips 13"w. From these strips, cut 4 **squares** 13" x 13".

6. **From light tan prints:**
   - For *each* of 16 baskets, cut 1 **large rectangle** 7" x 10" for triangle-squares and 1 **square** 2½" x 2½".

7. **From brown, gold, green, and rust prints and/or plaids:**
   - For *each* of the 16 baskets, cut 1 **large rectangle** 7" x 10" for triangle-squares.
   - For *each* of the 16 baskets, cut 1 strip 2⅞" x 11½". From this strip, cut 4 squares 2⅞" x 2⅞". Cut squares once diagonally to make 8 **small triangles**. (For each basket, you will need 7 and have 1 left over.)
   - Follow **Preparing Appliqué Pieces**, page 149, and use patterns, pages 139 and 141, to cut the following appliqué pieces:

A —	28	**J** —	8 (4 in reverse)
B —	94	**K** —	8 (4 in reverse)
C —	20	**L** —	4
D —	20	**M** —	4
E —	14	**N** —	4
F —	14	**O** —	4
G —	8	**P** —	4
H —	8	**Q** —	4
I —	8	**R** —	16

8. **From gold print for medallion borders:**
   - Cut 4 selvage-to-selvage strips 1¼"w. From these strips, cut 2 **short medallion borders** 1¼" x 24½" and 2 **long medallion borders** 1¼" x 26".

9. **From remaining scraps of brown, gold, green, rust, and light tan prints and/or plaids:**
   - Cut 72 squares 3⅞" x 3⅞". Cut squares once diagonally to make a total of 144 **random triangles**.

ASSEMBLING THE QUILT TOP
Follow Piecing and Pressing, page 146, to make quilt top.

1. To make triangle-squares, place 1 brown, gold, green, or rust **large rectangle** and 1 light tan print **large rectangle** right sides together. Referring to **Fig. 1**, follow Steps 1 - 3 of **Making Triangle-Squares**, page 147, to draw a grid of 6 squares 2⅞" x 2⅞". Referring to **Fig. 2** for stitching direction, follow Steps 4 - 6 of **Making Triangle-Squares** to complete 12 **triangle-squares**. (For each basket, you will need 9 triangle-squares and have 3 left over.) Repeat with remaining **large rectangles** to make **triangle-squares** for 16 baskets.

Fig. 1

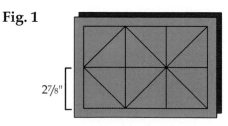

Fig. 2

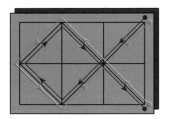

triangle-square (make 12)

2. Assemble 9 **triangle-squares**, 5 **small triangles**, and 1 **square** to make **Rows A**, **B**, **C**, **D**, and **E**. Assemble **Rows** to make **Unit 1**. Make 16 **Unit 1's**.

Row A
Row B
Row C
Row D
Row E

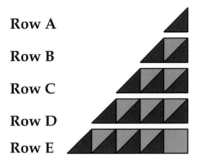

Unit 1 (make 16)

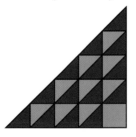

3. Assemble 1 **small triangle** and 1 **rectangle** to make **Unit 2**. Make 16 **Unit 2's**. Assemble 1 **rectangle** and 1 **small triangle** to make **Unit 3**. Make 16 **Unit 3's**.

Unit 2 (make 16)   **Unit 3** (make 16)

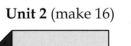   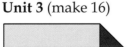

4. Assemble 1 **Unit 1**, 1 **Unit 2**, and 1 **Unit 3** to make **Unit 4**. Make 16 **Unit 4's**.

Unit 4 (make 16)

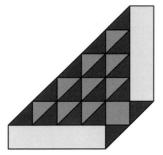

5. For basket handles, refer to **Quilt Top Diagram**, page 140, and follow **Almost Invisible Appliqué**, page 149, to stitch **R** appliqué pieces to **large triangles**, making sure handle ends extend into seam allowances.

6. Assemble 1 **large triangle**, 1 **Unit 4**, and 1 **medium triangle** to make **Basket Block**. Make 16 **Basket Blocks**.

Basket Block (make 16)

7. Assemble 4 **Basket Blocks** to make center medallion of quilt top. Sew **short medallion borders** to opposite edges of medallion. Sew **long medallion borders** to remaining edges of medallion to make **Unit 5**.

Unit 5 (make 1)

137

8. Assemble 2 **random triangles** to make **random triangle-square**. Make 60 **random triangle-squares**.

random triangle-square (make 60)

9. Assemble 15 **random triangle-squares** and 6 **random triangles** to make **Unit 6**. Make 4 **Unit 6's**.

Unit 6 (make 4)

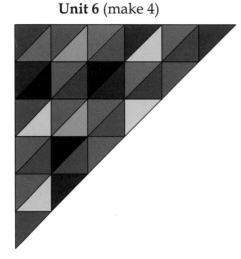

10. Assemble **Unit 6's** and **Unit 5** to make **Unit 7**.

Unit 7

11. Follow **Almost Invisible Appliqué**, page 149, to stitch appliqué pieces to **squares**. Trim **squares** to 12¹/₂" x 12¹/₂" to complete 4 **Appliquéd Blocks**.

Appliquéd Block (make 4)

12. Referring to **Quilt Top Diagram**, page 140, assemble remaining **Basket Blocks**, **Appliquéd Blocks**, and **Unit 7** to complete center section of quilt top.
13. Fold 1 **bias strip** in half lengthwise with *wrong* sides together; do not press. Stitch ¹/₄" from long raw edge to form a tube; trim seam allowance to ¹/₈". Place bias pressing bar inside 1 end of tube. Center seam and press as you move bar down length of tube. Repeat with remaining **bias strips** to make 4 **vines**.
14. Referring to **Quilt Top Diagram**, page 140, follow **Almost Invisible Appliqué**, page 149, to stitch 2 **vines** to each **border panel** with **vines** meeting in center (**Fig. 3**).

Fig. 3

15. Follow **Almost Invisible Appliqué**, page 149, to stitch remaining appliqué pieces to **border panels** to complete **Appliquéd Borders**.
16. Sew **Appliquéd Borders** to top and bottom of center section of quilt top.
17. Follow **Adding Squared Borders**, page 151, to attach **side**, then **top** and **bottom inner borders**. Repeat with **outer borders** to complete **Quilt Top**.

COMPLETING THE QUILT

1. Follow **Quilting**, page 152, to mark, layer, and quilt, using **Quilting Diagram** as a suggestion. Our quilt is hand quilted using **Vine** and **Leaf Quilting Patterns** and **Scroll Quilting Pattern**, page 141.
2. Cut a 34" square of binding fabric. Follow **Binding**, page 155, to bind quilt using 2½"w bias binding with mitered corners.

Quilting Diagram

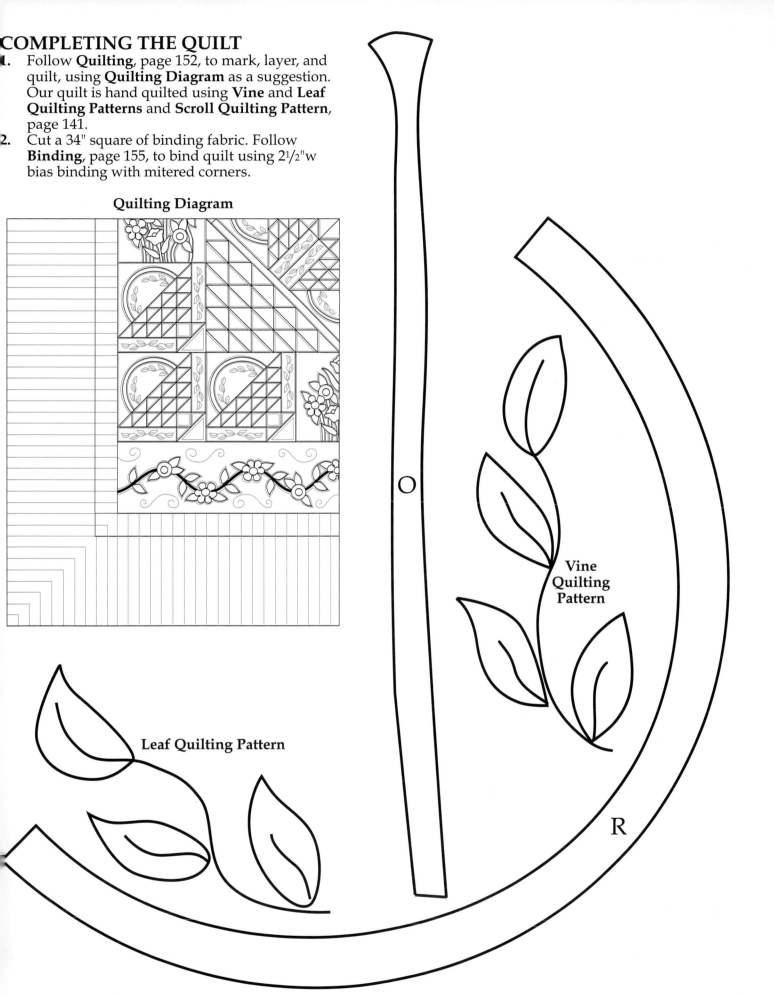

O

Vine
Quilting
Pattern

Leaf Quilting Pattern

R

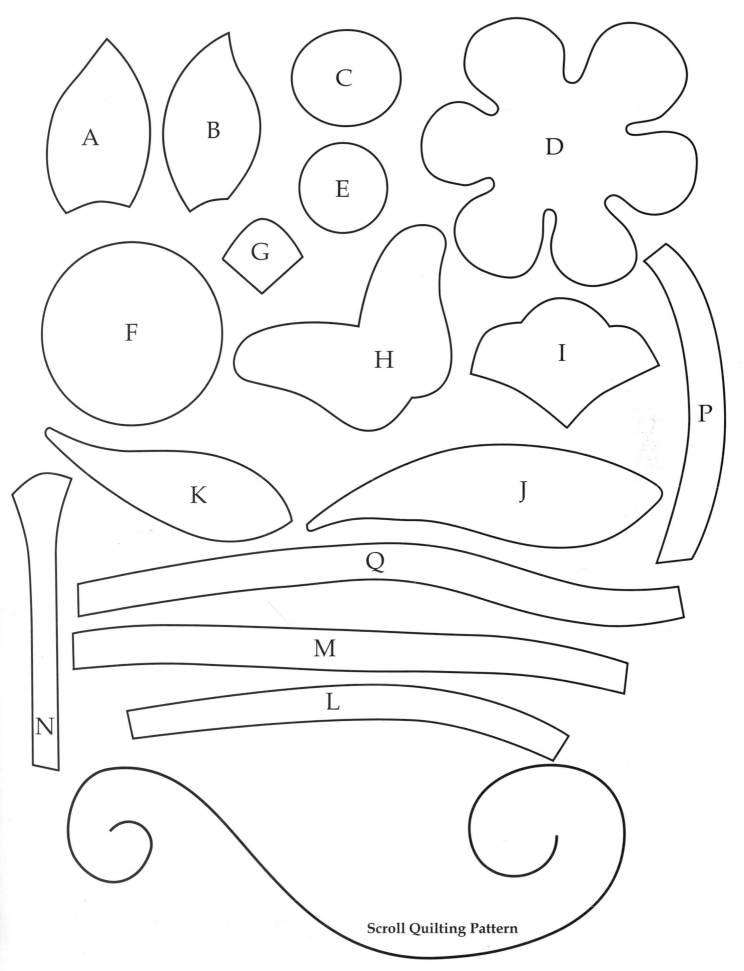

Scroll Quilting Pattern

GENERAL INSTRUCTIONS

Complete instructions are given for making each of the quilts and accompanying projects shown in this book. Skill levels indicated for quilts and wall hangings may help you choose the right project for you. To make your quilting easier and more enjoyable, we encourage you to carefully read all of these general instructions, study the color photographs, and familiarize yourself with the individual project instructions before beginning a project.

QUILTING SUPPLIES

This list includes all the tools you need for basic quick-method quiltmaking, plus additional supplies used for special techniques. Unless otherwise specified, all items may be found in your favorite fabric store or quilt shop.

Batting — Batting is most commonly available in polyester, cotton, or a polyester/cotton blend. See **Quick Tip**, page 133, for more information about batting.

Cutting mat — A cutting mat is a special mat designed to be used with a rotary cutter. A mat that measures approximately 18" x 24" is a good size for most cutting.

Eraser — A soft white fabric eraser or white art eraser may be used to remove pencil marks from fabric. Do not use a colored eraser, as the dye may discolor fabric.

Iron — An iron with both steam and dry settings and a smooth, clean soleplate is necessary for proper pressing.

Marking tools — There are many different types of marking tools available (see **Marking Quilting Lines**, page 152). A silver quilter's pencil is a good marker for both light and dark fabrics.

Masking Tape — Two widths of masking tape, 1"w and ¼"w, are helpful to have on hand when quilting. The 1"w tape is used to secure the backing fabric to a flat surface when layering the quilt. The ¼"w tape may be used as a guide when outline quilting.

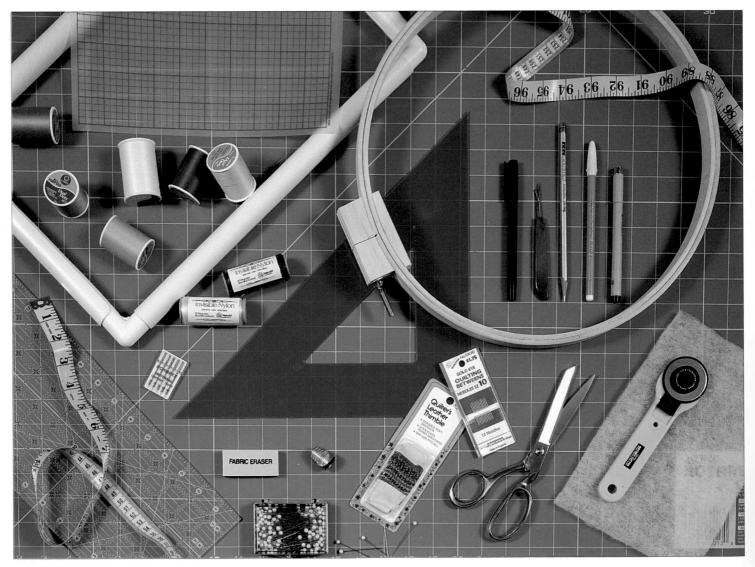

Needles — Two types of needles, betweens and sharps, are used for hand sewing. *Betweens*, used for quilting, are short and strong for stitching through layered fabric and batting. Beginning quilters may wish to try a size 8 or 9 needle. *Sharps* are longer, thinner needles used for basting and other hand sewing. For *sewing machine needles*, we recommend size 10 to 14 or 70 to 90 universal (sharp-pointed) needles made for woven fabrics.

Permanent fine-point marker — A permanent marker is used to mark templates and stencils and to sign and date quilts. Test marker on fabric to make sure it will not bleed or wash out.

Pins — Straight pins made especially for quilting are extra long with large, round heads. Some quilters prefer extra-fine dressmaker's silk pins.

Quilting hoop or frame — Quilting hoops and frames are designed to securely hold the 3 layers of a quilt together while you quilt. Many different types and sizes are available, including round and oval wooden hoops, frames made of rigid plastic pipe, and large floor frames made of either material. A 14" or 16" hoop allows you to quilt in your lap and makes your quilting portable.

Rotary cutter — The rotary cutter is the essential tool for quick-method quilting techniques. The cutter consists of a round, sharp blade mounted on a handle with a retractable blade guard for safety. It should be used only with a cutting mat and rotary cutting ruler. Two sizes are generally available; we recommend the larger (45 mm) size.

Rotary cutting rulers — A rotary cutting ruler is a thick, clear acrylic ruler made specifically for use with a rotary cutter. It should have accurate 1/8" crosswise and lengthwise markings and markings for 45° and 60° angles. A 6" x 24" ruler is a good size for most cutting. An additional 6" x 12" ruler or 12½" square ruler is helpful when cutting wider pieces. Many specialty rulers are available that make specific cutting tasks faster and easier.

Scissors — Although most cutting will be done with a rotary cutter, sharp, high-quality scissors are still needed for some cutting. A separate pair of scissors for cutting paper and plastic is recommended. Smaller scissors are handy for clipping threads.

Seam ripper — A good seam ripper with a fine point is useful for removing stitching.

Sewing machine — A sewing machine that produces a good, even straight stitch is all that is necessary for most quilting. Clean and oil your machine often and keep the tension set properly. Zigzag stitch capability is necessary for Almost Invisible Appliqué. Blindstitch with variable stitch width capability is required for Mock Hand Appliqué.

Stabilizer — Commercially made non-woven material or paper stabilizer is placed behind background fabric when stitching appliqués in place, then removed after stitching is complete. Water-soluble stabilizer is used to prepare appliqué pieces for Mock Hand Appliqué.

Tape measure — A flexible 120" long tape measure is helpful for measuring a quilt top before adding borders.

Template material — Sheets of translucent plastic, often pre-marked with a grid, are made especially for making templates and quilting stencils.

Thimble — A thimble is necessary when hand quilting. Thimbles are available in metal, plastic, or leather and in many sizes and styles. Choose a thimble that fits well and is comfortable.

Thread — Several types of thread are used for quiltmaking. *General-purpose* sewing thread is used for basting, piecing, and some appliquéing. Buy high-quality cotton or cotton-covered polyester thread in light and dark neutrals, such as ecru and grey, for your basic supplies. *Quilting* thread is stronger than general-purpose sewing thread, and some brands have a coating to make them slide more easily through the quilt layers. Some machine appliqué projects in this book use *transparent monofilament* (clear nylon) thread. Use a very fine, soft nylon thread that is not stiff or wiry. Choose clear nylon thread for white or light fabrics or smoke nylon thread for darker fabrics.

Triangle — A large plastic right-angle triangle (available in art and office supply stores) is useful in rotary cutting for making first cuts to "square up" raw edges of fabric and for checking to see that cuts remain at right angles to fold.

Walking foot — A walking foot or even-feed foot is needed for straight-line machine quilting. This special foot will help all 3 layers of the quilt move at the same rate over the feed dogs to provide a smoother quilted project.

FABRICS

SELECTING FABRICS

For many quilters, choosing fabrics for a new quilt project is one of the most challenging and fun parts of quilting. Photographs of our quilts are excellent guides for choosing the colors for your quilt. You may choose to duplicate the colors in the photograph, or you may use the same light, medium, and dark values in completely different color families. When you change the light and dark value placement in a quilt block, you may come up with a surprising new creation. The most important lesson to learn about fabrics and color is to choose fabrics you love. When you combine several fabrics you are simply crazy about in a quilt, you are sure to be happy with the results!

The yardage requirements listed for each project are based on 45" wide fabric with a "usable" width of 42" after shrinkage and trimming selvages. Your actual "usable" width may be wider, and it will probably vary slightly from fabric to fabric. Our yardage lengths should be adequate for occasional resquaring of fabric when many cuts are required, but it never hurts to buy a little more fabric for insurance against cutting errors or to have on hand for making coordinating projects.

Choose high-quality, medium-weight, 100% cotton fabrics such as broadcloth or calico. All-cotton fabrics hold a crease better, fray less, and are easier to quilt than cotton/polyester blends. All the fabrics for a quilt should be of comparable weight and weave. Check the end of the fabric bolt for fiber content and width.

PREPARING FABRICS

All fabrics should be washed, dried, and pressed before cutting.

1. To check colorfastness before washing, cut a small piece of the fabric and place in a glass of hot water with a little detergent. Leave fabric in the water for a few minutes. Remove from water and blot fabric with white paper towels. If any color bleeds onto the towels, wash the fabric separately with warm water and detergent, then rinse until the water runs clear. If fabric continues to bleed, choose another fabric.
2. Unfold yardage and separate fabrics by color. To help reduce raveling, use scissors to snip off small corners of fabric pieces (**Fig. 1**). Machine wash in warm water with a small amount of mild laundry detergent. Do not use fabric softener. Rinse well and then dry fabrics in the dryer, checking long fabric lengths occasionally to make sure they are not tangling.

Fig. 1

3. To make ironing easier, remove fabrics from dryer while they are slightly damp. Refold each fabric lengthwise (as it was on the bolt) with wrong sides together and matching selvages. If necessary, adjust slightly at selvages so that fold lies flat. Press each fabric with a steam iron set on "Cotton."

ROTARY CUTTING

*Based on the idea that you can easily cut strips of fabric and then cut those strips into smaller pieces, rotary cutting has brought speed and accuracy to quiltmaking. Observe safety precautions when using the rotary cutter since it is extremely sharp. Develop a habit of retracting the blade guard **just before** making a cut and closing it **immediately afterward**, before laying down the cutter.*

1. Follow **Preparing Fabrics** to wash, dry, and press fabrics.
2. Most strips are cut from the selvage-to-selvage width of a length of fabric. Place fabric on the cutting mat as shown in **Fig. 2** with the fold of the fabric toward you. To straighten the uneven fabric edge, make the first "squaring up" cut by placing the right edge of the rotary cutting ruler over the left raw edge of the fabric. Place right-angle triangle with the lower edge carefully aligned with the fold and the left edge against the ruler (**Fig. 2**). Hold the ruler firmly with your left hand, placing your little finger off the left edge of the ruler to anchor it. Remove the triangle, pick up the rotary cutter, and retract the blade guard. Using a smooth, downward motion, make the cut by running the blade of the rotary cutter firmly along the right edge of the ruler (**Fig. 3**). **Always** cut in a direction **away** from your body and **immediately** close the blade guard after each cut.

Fig. 2

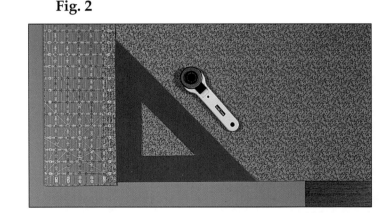

Fig. 3

3. After squaring up, cut the strips required for the project. Place the ruler over the cut edge of the fabric, aligning desired marking on the ruler with the cut edge of the fabric (**Fig. 4**). When cutting several strips from a single piece of fabric, it is important to occasionally use the ruler and triangle to ensure that cuts are still at a perfect right angle to the fold. If not, repeat Step 2 to straighten.

Fig. 4

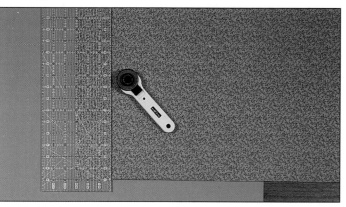

4. To square up selvage ends of a strip before cutting pieces, refer to **Fig. 5** and place folded strip on mat with selvage ends to your right. Aligning a horizontal marking on ruler with 1 long edge of strip, use rotary cutter to trim off selvage to make end of strip square and even (**Fig. 5**). Turn strip (or entire mat) so that cut end is to your left before making subsequent cuts.

Fig. 5

5. Pieces such as rectangles and squares can now be cut from strips. (Cutting other shapes like diamonds is discussed in individual project instructions.) Usually strips remain folded, and pieces are cut in pairs after ends of strips are squared up. To cut squares or rectangles from a strip, place ruler over left end of strip, aligning desired marking on ruler with cut end of strip.

To ensure perfectly square cuts, align a horizontal marking on ruler with 1 long edge of strip (**Fig. 6**). Make cut as in Step 2.

Fig. 6

6. After some practice, you may want to try stacking up to 6 fabric layers when making cuts. When stacking strips, match long cut edges and follow Step 4 to square up ends of strip stack. Carefully turn stack (or entire mat) so that squared-up ends are at your left before making subsequent cuts. After cutting, check accuracy of pieces. Some shapes, such as diamonds, are more difficult to cut accurately in stacks.

7. In some cases, strips will be sewn together into strip sets before being cut into smaller units. When cutting a strip set, align a seam in strip set with a horizontal marking on the ruler to maintain square cuts (**Fig. 7**). We do not recommend stacking strip sets for rotary cutting.

Fig. 7

8. Most borders for quilts in this book are cut along the more stable lengthwise grain to minimize wavy edges caused by stretching. To remove selvages before cutting lengthwise strips, place fabric on mat with selvages to your left and squared-up end at bottom of mat. Placing ruler over selvage and using squared-up edge instead of fold, follow Step 2 to cut away selvages as you did raw edges (**Fig. 8**). After making a cut the length of the mat, move the next section to be cut onto the mat. Repeat until you have removed selvages from required length of fabric.

Fig. 8

9. After removing selvages, place ruler over left edge of fabric, aligning desired marking on ruler with cut edge of fabric. Make cuts as in Step 3. After each cut, move next section of fabric onto mat as in Step 8.

TEMPLATE CUTTING

Our full-sized templates have two lines: a solid cutting line and a dashed line showing the ¼" seam allowance.

1. To make a template from a whole pattern, use a permanent fine-point marker to carefully trace pattern onto template plastic, making sure to transfer all alignment and grain line markings. Cut out template along inner edge of drawn line. Check template against original pattern for accuracy.
2. To make a template from a half pattern, use a ruler to draw a line down the center of a sheet of template plastic. Match grey line of pattern to drawn line on plastic. Trace pattern onto plastic. Turn plastic over and trace pattern again to complete. Cut out template as in Step 1.
3. To make a template from a one-quarter pattern, use a ruler to draw a line down the center of a sheet of template plastic. Turn plastic 90° and draw a line down the center, perpendicular to

the first line. Match grey lines of pattern to intersection of lines on plastic. Trace pattern. Turn plastic and trace pattern in remaining corners. Cut out template as in Step 1.

4. To use a template, place template on wrong side of fabric (unless indicated otherwise), aligning grain line on template with grain of fabric and use a sharp fabric marking pencil to draw around template. Transfer all alignment markings to fabric. Cut out fabric piece using scissors or rotary cutter and ruler.

PIECING AND PRESSING

Precise cutting, followed by accurate piecing and careful pressing, will ensure that all the pieces of your quilt top fit together well.

PIECING

Set sewing machine stitch length for approximately 11 stitches per inch. Use a new, sharp needle suited for medium-weight woven fabric.

Use general-purpose sewing thread (not quilting thread) in the needle and in the bobbin. Stitch first on a scrap of fabric to check upper and bobbin thread tension and make any adjustments necessary.

For good results, it is **essential** that you stitch with an **accurate ¼" seam allowance**. On many sewing machines, the measurement from the needle to the outer edge of the presser foot is ¼". If this is the case with your machine, the presser foot is your best guide. If not, measure ¼" from the needle and mark with a piece of masking tape. Special presser feet that are exactly ¼" wide are also available for most sewing machines.

When piecing, **always** place pieces **right sides together** and **match raw edges**; pin if necessary. (If using straight pins, remove the pins just before they reach the sewing machine needle.)

Chain Piecing

Chain piecing whenever possible will make your work go faster and will usually result in more accurate piecing. Stack the pieces you will be sewing beside your machine in the order you will need them and in a position that will allow you to easily pick them up. Pick up each pair of pieces, carefully place them together as they will be sewn, and feed them into the machine one after the other. Stop between each pair only long enough to pick up the next and don't cut thread between pairs (**Fig. 9**). After all pieces are sewn, cut threads, press, and go on to the next step, chain piecing when possible.

Fig. 9

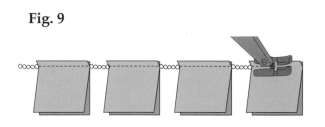

Sewing Strip Sets

When there are several strips to assemble into a strip set, first sew the strips together into pairs, then sew the pairs together to form the strip set. To help avoid distortion, sew 1 seam in 1 direction and then sew the next seam in the opposite direction (**Fig. 10**).

Fig. 10

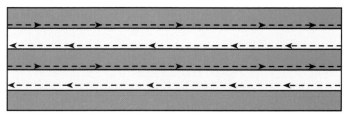

Sewing Across Seam Intersections

When sewing across the intersection of 2 seams, place pieces right sides together and match seams, making sure seam allowances are pressed in opposite directions (**Fig. 11**). To prevent fabric from shifting, you may wish to pin in place.

Fig. 11

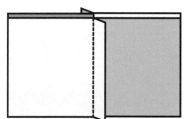

Sewing Sharp Points

To ensure sharp points when joining triangular or diagonal pieces, stitch across the center of the "X" (shown in pink) formed on the wrong side by previous seams (**Fig. 12**).

Fig. 12

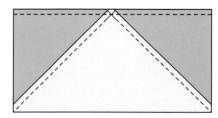

Sewing Bias Seams

Care should be used in handling and stitching bias edges, since they stretch easily. After sewing the seam, carefully press seam allowances to 1 side, making sure not to stretch the fabric.

Making Triangle-Squares

The grid method for making triangle-squares is faster and more accurate than cutting and sewing individual triangles. Stitching before cutting the triangle-squares apart also prevents stretching the bias edges.

1. Follow project instructions to cut rectangles or squares of fabric for making triangle-squares. Place the indicated pieces right sides together and press.
2. On the wrong side of the lighter fabric, draw a grid of squares similar to that shown in **Fig. 13**. The size and number of squares will be given in the project instructions.

Fig. 13

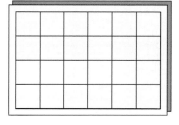

3. Following the example given in the project instructions, draw 1 diagonal line through each square in the grid (**Fig. 14**).

Fig. 14

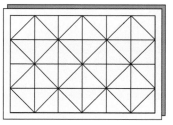

4. Stitch ¼" on each side of all diagonal lines. In some cases, stitching may be done in a single continuous line. Project instructions include a diagram similar to **Fig. 15** which shows stitching lines and the direction of the stitching.

Fig. 15

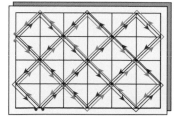

5. Use rotary cutter and ruler to cut along all drawn lines of the grid. Each square of the grid will yield 2 triangle-squares (**Fig. 16**).

Fig. 16

6. Carefully press triangle-squares open, pressing seam allowance toward darker fabric. Trim off points of seam allowances that extend beyond edges of triangle-square (see **Fig. 21**).

Working with Diamond Shapes

Piecing diamonds requires special handling. For best results, carefully follow the steps below to assemble the diamond sections of a block.

1. When sewing 2 diamond pieces together, place pieces right sides together, carefully matching edges; pin. Mark a small dot 1/4" from corner of 1 piece as shown in **Fig. 17**. Stitch pieces together in the direction shown in **Fig. 17**, stopping at center of dot and backstitching.

Fig. 17

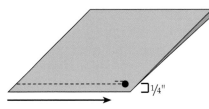

2. To add corner squares and side triangles to diamond sections, mark corner to be set in with a small dot (**Fig. 18**). Match right sides and pin the square or triangle to the diamond on the left. Stitch seam from the outer edge to the dot, backstitching at each end (**Fig. 19**).

Fig. 18

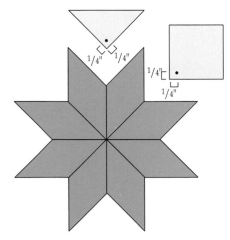

Fig. 19

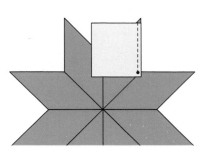

3. To sew the second seam, pivot the added square or triangle to match raw edges of next diamond. Pin and sew as before, beginning with the needle in the hole of the last stitch taken and sewing to the edge of the fabric (**Fig. 20**).

Fig. 20

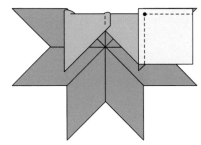

Trimming Seam Allowances

When sewing with diamond or triangle pieces, some seam allowances may extend beyond the edges of the sewn pieces. Trim these "dog ears" even with pieces to which they are joined (**Fig. 21**).

Fig. 21

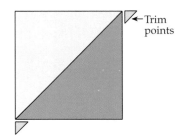

PRESSING

Use a steam iron set on "Cotton" for all pressing. Press as you sew, taking care to prevent small folds along seamlines. Seam allowances are almost always pressed to one side, usually toward the darker fabric. However, to reduce bulk it may occasionally be necessary to press seam allowances toward the lighter fabric or even to press them open. In order to prevent a dark fabric seam allowance from showing through a light fabric, trim the darker seam allowance slightly narrower than the lighter seam allowance.

APPLIQUÉ

PREPARING APPLIQUÉ PIECES

*Patterns are printed in reverse to enable you to use our speedy method of preparing appliqués. This method can be used when securing appliqués with **Almost Invisible Appliqué** or **blanket stitching**.*

1. Place paper-backed fusible web, web side down, over appliqué pattern. Use a pencil to trace pattern onto paper side of web as many times as indicated in project instructions for a single fabric. Repeat for additional patterns and fabrics.
2. Follow manufacturer's instructions to fuse traced patterns to wrong side of fabrics. Do not remove paper backing.
3. Some projects may have pieces that are given as measurements (such as a 2" x 4" rectangle) instead of drawn patterns. Fuse web to wrong side of fabrics indicated for these pieces.
4. Use scissors to cut out appliqué pieces along traced lines; use rotary cutter and ruler to cut out appliqué pieces given as measurements. Remove paper backing from all pieces.

ALMOST INVISIBLE APPLIQUÉ

This method of machine appliqué is an adaptation of satin stitch appliqué that uses clear nylon thread to secure the appliqué pieces. Appliqués are prepared using the method described above.

1. Referring to diagram and/or photo, arrange appliqués on the background fabric and follow manufacturer's instructions to fuse in place.
2. Place a stabilizer, such as paper or any of the commercially available products, on wrong side of background fabric before stitching appliqués in place.
3. Thread sewing machine with transparent monofilament thread; use general-purpose thread that matches background fabric in bobbin.
4. Set sewing machine for a very narrow (approximately 1/16") zigzag stitch and a short stitch length. You may find that loosening the top tension slightly will yield a smoother stitch.
5. Begin by stitching 2 or 3 stitches in place (drop feed dogs or set stitch length at 0) to anchor thread. Most of the zigzag stitch should be done on the appliqué with the right edge of the stitch falling at the very outside edge of the appliqué (**Fig. 22**). Stitch over all exposed raw edges of appliqué pieces.

Fig. 22

6. *(Note: Dots on **Figs. 23 - 28** indicate where to leave needle in fabric when pivoting.)* For **outside corners**, stitch just past the corner, stopping with the needle in **background** fabric (**Fig. 23**). Raise presser foot. Pivot project, lower presser foot, and stitch adjacent side (**Fig. 24**).

Fig. 23   **Fig. 24**

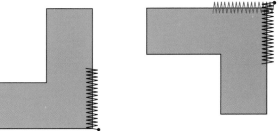

7. For **inside corners**, stitch just past the corner, stopping with the needle in **appliqué** fabric (**Fig. 25**). Raise presser foot. Pivot project, lower presser foot, and stitch adjacent side (**Fig. 26**).

Fig. 25   **Fig. 26**

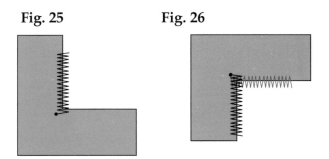

8. When stitching **outside** curves, stop with needle in **background** fabric. Raise presser foot and pivot project as needed. Lower presser foot and continue stitching, pivoting as often as necessary to follow curve (**Fig. 27**).

Fig. 27

9. When stitching **inside** curves, stop with needle in **appliqué** fabric. Raise presser foot and pivot project as needed. Lower presser foot and continue stitching, pivoting as often as necessary to follow curve (**Fig. 28**).

Fig. 28

10. End stitching by sewing 2 or 3 stitches in place to anchor thread. Trim thread ends close to fabric.
11. Carefully tear away stabilizer.

MOCK HAND APPLIQUÉ

*This technique uses the blindstitch on your sewing machine to achieve a look that closely resembles traditional hand appliqué. Appliqués are made using an updated method that allows you to use your sewing machine and water-soluble stabilizer to make quick and accurate appliqués with smooth, turned-under edges. The appliqués are then machine stitched to the background fabric. For best results using mock hand appliqué, your sewing machine **must** have blindstitch capability with a variable stitch width. If your blindstitch width cannot be adjusted, you may still wish to try this technique to see if you are happy with the results. Some sewing machines have a narrower blindstitch width than others.*

1. Follow project instructions to prepare appliqué pieces using water-soluble stabilizer.
2. Thread needle of sewing machine with transparent monofilament thread; use general-purpose thread in bobbin in a color to match background fabric.
3. Set sewing machine for narrow blind hem stitch (just wide enough to catch 2 or 3 threads of the appliqué) and a very short stitch length (20 - 30 stitches per inch).
4. Arrange appliqué pieces on background fabric (or other appliqués) as described in project instructions. Use pins or hand baste to secure.

5. (*Note*: Follow Steps 6 - 9 of **Almost Invisible Appliqué**, page 149, for needle position when pivoting.) Sew around edges of each appliqué so that the straight stitches fall on the background fabric very near the appliqué and the "hem" stitches barely catch the folded edge of the appliqué (**Fig. 29**).

Fig. 29

6. It is not necessary to backstitch at beginning or end of stitching. End stitching by sewing 1/4" over the first stitches. Trim thread ends close to fabric.
7. To reduce bulk, turn project over and use scissors to cut away background (or other appliqué) fabric approximately 1/4" inside stitching line of appliqué as shown in **Fig. 30**. You may also cut away any visible stabilizer.

Fig. 30

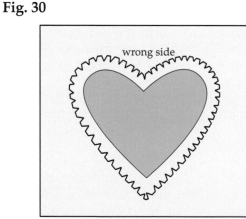

wrong side

8. When all appliquéing is complete, follow manufacturer's instructions to remove remaining stabilizer.

BORDERS

Borders cut along the lengthwise grain will lie flatter than borders cut along the crosswise grain. In most cases, our instructions for cutting borders for bed-size quilts include an extra 2" of length at each end for "insurance"; borders will be trimmed after measuring completed center section of quilt top.

ADDING SQUARED BORDERS

1. Mark the center of each edge of quilt top.
2. Squared borders are usually added to top and bottom, then side edges of the center section of a quilt top. To add top border, measure across center of quilt top to determine length of border (**Fig. 31**). Trim border to the determined length.

Fig. 31

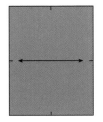

3. Mark center of 1 long edge of border. Matching center marks and raw edges, pin border to quilt top, easing in any fullness; stitch.
4. Repeat Steps 2 and 3 to add bottom border to quilt top.
5. Measure center of quilt top (including attached borders) to determine length of side borders. Repeat Steps 2 and 3 to add side borders to quilt top (**Fig. 32**).

Fig. 32

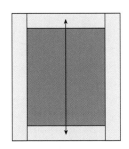

ADDING MITERED BORDERS

1. Mark the center of each edge of quilt top.
2. Mark center of 1 long edge of top border. Measure across center of quilt top (see **Fig. 31**). Matching center marks and raw edges, pin border to center of quilt top edge. From center of border, measure out 1/2 the width of the quilt top in both directions and mark. Match marks on border with corners of quilt top and pin. Easing in any fullness, pin border to quilt top between center and corners. Sew border to quilt top, beginning and ending seams **exactly** 1/4" from each corner of quilt top and backstitching at beginning and end of stitching (**Fig. 33**).

Fig. 33

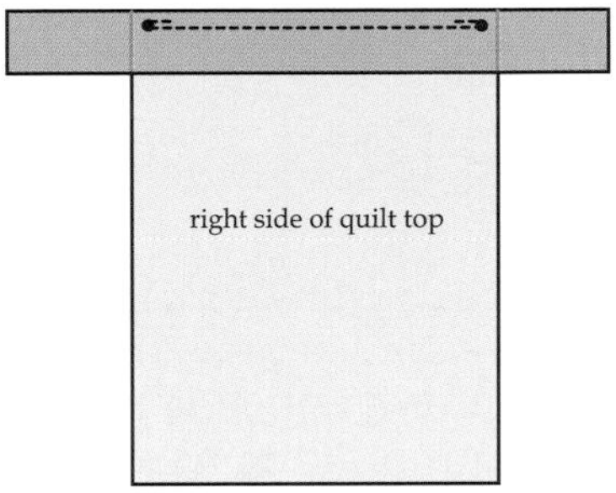

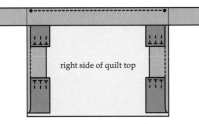

right side of quilt top

3. Repeat Step 2 to sew bottom, then side borders, to center section of quilt top. To temporarily move first 2 borders out of the way, fold and pin ends as shown in **Fig. 34**.

Fig. 34

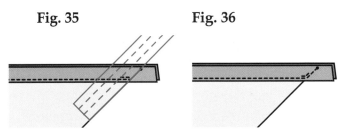

right side of quilt top

4. Fold 1 corner of quilt top diagonally with right sides together and matching edges. Use rotary cutting ruler to mark stitching line as shown in **Fig. 35**. Pin borders together along drawn line. Sew on drawn line, backstitching at beginning and end of stitching (**Fig. 36**).

Fig. 35   **Fig. 36**

5. Turn mitered corner right side up. Check to see that there is not a gap at the inner end of the seam and that corner does not pucker.
6. Trim seam allowances to 1/4"; press to 1 side.
7. Repeat Steps 4 - 6 to miter each remaining corner.

QUILTING

Quilting holds the 3 layers (top, batting, and backing) of the quilt together and may be done by hand or machine. Our project instructions tell you which method is used on our quilts and show you quilting diagrams that can be used as suggestions for marking quilting designs. Because marking, layering, and quilting are interrelated and may be done in different orders depending on circumstances, please read this entire section, pages 152 - 154, before beginning the quilting process on your project.

TYPES OF QUILTING

In the Ditch
Quilting very close to a seamline (**Fig. 37**) or appliqué (**Fig. 38**) is called "in the ditch" quilting. This type of quilting does not need to be marked and is indicated on our quilting diagrams with blue lines close to seamlines. When quilting in the ditch, quilt on the side **opposite** the seam allowance.

Fig. 37

Fig. 38

Outline Quilting
Quilting approximately 1/4" from a seam or appliqué is called "outline" quilting (**Fig. 39**). This type of quilting is indicated on our quilting diagrams by blue lines a short distance from seamlines. Outline quilting may be marked, or you may place 1/4"w masking tape along seamlines and quilt along the opposite edge of the tape. (Do not leave tape on quilt longer than necessary, since it may leave an adhesive residue.)

Fig. 39

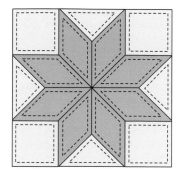

Ornamental Quilting
Quilting decorative lines or designs is called "ornamental" quilting (**Fig. 40**). Ornamental quilting is indicated on our quilting diagrams by blue lines. This type of quilting should be marked before you baste quilt layers together.

Fig. 40

MARKING QUILTING LINES
Lead, silver, and white fabric marking pencils; various types of chalk markers; and fabric marking pens with inks that disappear with exposure to air or water are readily available and work well for different applications. Lead pencils work well on light-colored fabric, but marks may be difficult to remove. White pencils work well on dark-colored fabric, and silver pencils show up well on many colors. Keep pencils sharp to ensure accuracy. Press down only as hard as necessary to make a visible line. Marks need to remain on the fabric until you are finished quilting, but should be relatively easy to remove after stitching is complete.

When you choose to mark your quilt, whether before or after the layers are basted together, is also a factor in deciding which marking tool to use. If you mark with chalk or a chalk pencil, handling the quilt during basting may rub off the markings. Intricate or ornamental designs may not be practical to mark as you quilt; mark these designs before basting using a more durable marker.

To choose marking tools, take all these factors into consideration and **test** different markers **on scrap fabric** until you find the one that gives the desired result.

USING QUILTING STENCILS

A wide variety of pre-cut quilting stencils, as well as entire books of quilting patterns, are available at your local quilt shop or fabric store. Our book includes patterns of some original quilting designs, as well as some classics you might like to use on your project. Wherever you draw your quilting inspiration from, using a stencil makes it easier to mark intricate or repetitive designs on your quilt top.

1. To make a stencil from a pattern, center template plastic over pattern and use a permanent marker to trace pattern onto plastic.
2. To make stencils from a half pattern or one-quarter pattern, follow Step 2 or 3 of **Template Cutting**, page 146.
3. Use a craft knife with a single or double blade to cut narrow slits along traced lines (**Fig. 41**).

Fig. 41

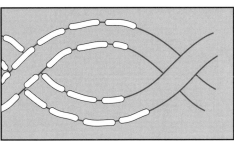

4. Use desired marking tool and stencil to mark quilting lines.

PREPARING BACKING AND BATTING

To allow for the quilt top shifting slightly during quilting, the backing and batting should be approximately 4" larger on all sides for a bed-size quilt top or approximately 2" larger on all sides for a wall hanging. Yardage requirements listed for quilt backings are calculated for 45"w fabric. If you are making a bed-size quilt, using 90"w or 108"w fabric for the backing may eliminate piecing. To piece a backing using 45"w fabric, use the following instructions.

1. Measure length and width of quilt top; add 8" (4" for a wall hanging) to each measurement.
2. If quilt top is 76"w or less, cut backing fabric into 2 lengths slightly longer than the determined **length** measurement. Trim selvages. Place lengths with right sides facing and sew long edges together, forming a tube (**Fig. 42**). Match seams and press along 1 fold (**Fig. 43**). Cut along pressed fold to form a single piece (**Fig. 44**).

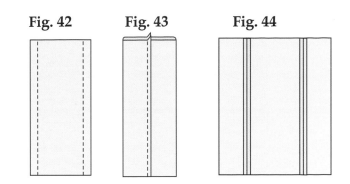

Fig. 42   **Fig. 43**   **Fig. 44**

3. If quilt top is more than 76"w, cut backing fabric into 3 lengths slightly longer than the determined **width** measurement. Trim selvages. Sew long edges together to form a single piece.
4. Trim to correct size, if necessary, and press seam allowances open.
5. Trim batting to same size as backing.

LAYERING THE QUILT

1. Examine wrong side of quilt top closely and trim any seam allowances and clip any threads that may show through the front of the quilt. Press quilt top.
2. If top is to be marked before layering, mark quilting lines on quilt top (see **Marking Quilting Lines**, page 152).
3. Place backing **wrong** side up on a flat surface. Use masking tape to tape backing to surface. Place batting on wrong side of backing fabric. Smooth batting gently, being careful not to stretch or tear. Center quilt top **right** side up on batting.
4. If hand quilting, begin in the center and work toward the outer edges to hand baste all layers together. Use long stitches and place basting lines approximately 4" apart (**Fig. 45**). Smooth fullness or wrinkles toward outer edges.

Fig. 45

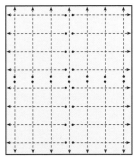

5. If machine quilting, use 1" brass or nickel-plated safety pins to "pin-baste" all layers together, spacing pins approximately 4" apart. Begin at the center and work toward the outer edges to secure all layers. If possible, place pins away from areas that will be quilted, although pins may be removed as needed when quilting.

HAND QUILTING

The quilting stitch is a basic running stitch that forms a broken line on the quilt top and backing. Stitches on the quilt top and backing should be straight and equal in length.

1. Secure center of quilt in hoop or frame. Check quilt top and backing to make sure they are smooth. To help prevent puckers, always begin quilting in the center of the quilt and work toward the outside edges.

2. Thread needle with an 18" - 20" length of quilting thread; knot 1 end. Using a thimble, insert needle into quilt top and batting approximately ½" from where you wish to begin quilting. Bring needle up at the point where you wish to begin (**Fig. 46**); when knot catches on quilt top, give thread a quick, short pull to "pop" knot through fabric into batting (**Fig. 47**).

Fig. 46

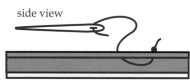
side view

Fig. 47

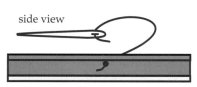
side view

3. Holding the needle with your sewing hand and placing your other hand underneath the quilt, use thimble to push the tip of the needle down through all layers. As soon as needle touches your finger underneath, use that finger to push only the tip of the needle back up through the layers to top of quilt. (The amount of the needle showing above the fabric determines the length of the quilting stitch.) Referring to **Fig. 48**, rock the needle up and down, taking 3 - 6 stitches before bringing the needle and thread completely through the layers. Check the back of the quilt to make sure stitches are going through all layers. When quilting through a seam allowance or quilting a curve or corner, you may need to take 1 stitch at a time.

Fig. 48

4. When you reach the end of your thread, knot thread close to the fabric and "pop" knot into batting; clip thread close to fabric. Try to keep stitches straight and even; with practice, stitches will become smaller.

5. Stop and move your hoop as often as necessary. You do not have to tie a knot every time you move your hoop; you may leave the thread dangling and pick it up again when you return to that part of the quilt.

MACHINE QUILTING

There are 2 types of machine quilting: straight-line and free-motion. The machine-quilted projects in this book utilize straight-line quilting, which requires a walking foot or even-feed foot. Use transparent monofilament thread if you want your quilting to "match" all your fabric. Other decorative threads, such as metallics and contrasting colored threads, can be used when you want the quilting lines to stand out more.

1. After pin-basting, decide which section of the quilt will have the longest continuous quilting line, oftentimes from center top to center bottom. Leaving the area exposed where you will place your first line of quilting, roll up each edge of the quilt, keeping fabrics smooth.

2. Thread the bobbin with general-purpose thread that matches the quilt backing. Do not use quilting thread. Thread the needle of your machine with transparent monofilament thread or desired decorative thread. Set the stitch length for 6 - 10 stitches per inch. Attach walking foot to sewing machine.

3. Start stitching at beginning of longest quilting line, using very short stitches to "lock" beginning stitches. Stitch across project, locking stitches at end of quilting line.

4. Continue machine quilting, locking all stitching lines at beginning and end and rerolling project as necessary.

BINDING

Binding encloses the raw edges of your quilt. The stretchiness of bias binding works well for binding projects with curves or rounded corners; it also tends to lie smooth and flat in any given circumstance. Binding may also be cut from the straight lengthwise or crosswise grain of the fabric. You will find that straight-grain binding works well for projects with straight edges.

PREPARING QUILT FOR BINDING

1. When you have finished quilting, remove all basting threads or safety pins.
2. Using a narrow zigzag stitch with a medium stitch length, machine stitch along all edges of quilt top through all layers. Trim batting and backing a scant ¼" larger than quilt top (**Fig. 49**).

Fig. 49

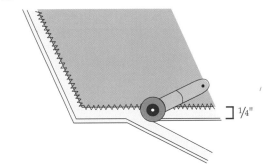

3. If you wish to attach a hanging sleeve to your quilt or wall hanging, follow **Making a Hanging Sleeve**, page 157, before attaching binding.

MAKING CONTINUOUS BIAS STRIP BINDING

Bias strips for binding can simply be cut and pieced to the desired length. However, when a long length of binding is needed, the "continuous" method is quick and accurate.

1. Cut a square from binding fabric the size indicated in the project instructions. Cut square in half diagonally to make 2 triangles.
2. With right sides together and using a ¼" seam allowance, sew triangles together (**Fig. 50**); press seam allowance open.

Fig. 50

3. On wrong side of fabric, draw lines the width specified in the project instructions, usually 2½" (**Fig. 51**). Cut off any remaining fabric less than this width.

Fig. 51

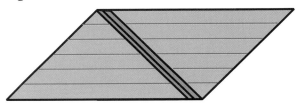

4. With right sides inside, bring short edges together to form a tube (**Fig. 52**).

Fig. 52

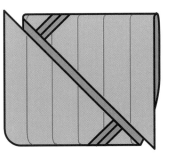

5. Match raw edges so that first drawn line of top section meets second drawn line of bottom section. Insert pins through drawn lines at the point where drawn lines intersect, making sure the pins go through intersections on both sides (**Fig. 53**). Carefully pin edges together. Using a ¼" seam allowance, sew edges together. Press seam allowance open.

Fig. 53

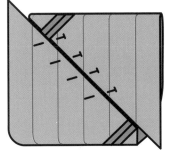

6. To cut continuous strip, begin cutting along first drawn line (**Fig. 54**). Continue cutting along drawn line around tube.

Fig. 54

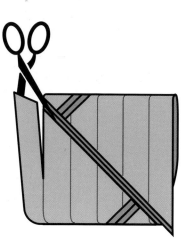

7. Trim each end of bias strip as shown in **Fig. 55**.

Fig. 55

8. Matching wrong sides and raw edges, press bias strip in half lengthwise to complete binding.

MAKING STRAIGHT-GRAIN BINDING

1. Measure each edge of quilt; add 3" to each measurement. Cut lengthwise or crosswise strips of binding fabric the width called for in the project instructions. Strips may be pieced to achieve the necessary length.
2. Matching wrong sides and raw edges, press strips in half lengthwise to complete binding.

ATTACHING BINDING WITH MITERED CORNERS

1. Press 1 end of binding diagonally (**Fig. 56**).

Fig. 56

2. Matching raw edges of binding to raw edge of quilt top and beginning with pressed end several inches from a corner, pin binding to right side of quilt along 1 side. Lay binding around quilt to make sure that seams in binding will not end up at a corner. Adjust placement if necessary.

3. When you reach the first corner, mark ¼" from corner of quilt (**Fig. 57**).

Fig. 57

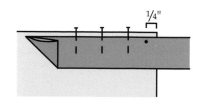

4. Using a ¼" seam allowance, sew binding to quilt, backstitching at beginning of stitching and when you reach the mark (**Fig. 58**). Lift needle out of fabric and clip thread.

Fig. 58

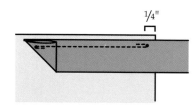

5. Fold binding as shown in **Figs. 59** and **60** and pin binding to adjacent side, matching raw edges. When you reach the next corner, mark ¼" from edge of quilt.

Fig. 59   **Fig. 60**

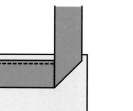 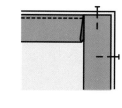

6. Backstitching at edge of quilt, sew pinned binding to quilt (**Fig. 61**); backstitch when you reach the next mark. Lift needle out of fabric and clip thread.

Fig. 61

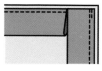

7. Repeat Steps 5 and 6 to continue sewing binding to quilt. Leaving a 2" overlap, trim excess binding. Stitch overlap in place.
8. On 1 edge of quilt, fold binding over to quilt backing and pin pressed edge in place, covering stitching line (**Fig. 62**). On adjacent side, fold binding over, forming a mitered corner (**Fig. 63**). Repeat to pin remainder of binding in place.

Fig. 62   **Fig. 63**

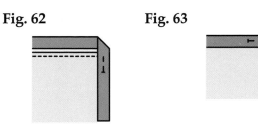

9. Blindstitch binding to backing.

ATTACHING BINDING WITH OVERLAPPED CORNERS

1. Matching raw edges and using a ¼" seam allowance, sew 1 binding length to 1 edge on right side of quilt; trim ends of binding even with quilt. Fold binding over to quilt backing and pin pressed edge in place, covering stitching line (**Fig. 64**); blindstitch binding to backing. Repeat for opposite edge of quilt.

Fig. 64

2. Leaving approximately 1½" at each end, stitch 1 binding length to 1 raw edge of quilt. Trim each end of binding ½" longer than bound edge. Fold each end of binding over to quilt backing (**Fig. 65**); pin in place. Repeat for remaining edge.

Fig. 65

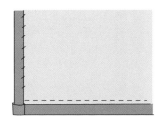

3. Fold binding over to quilt backing and blindstitch in place.

MAKING A HANGING SLEEVE

Attaching a hanging sleeve to the back of your wall hanging or quilt before the binding is added allows you to display your completed project on a wall.

1. Measure the width of the wall hanging and subtract 1". Cut a piece of fabric 7"w by the determined measurement.
2. Press short edges of fabric piece ¼" to wrong side; press edges ¼" to wrong side again and machine stitch in place.
3. Matching wrong sides, fold piece in half lengthwise to form a tube.
4. Matching raw edges, baste hanging sleeve to center top edge on back of wall hanging.
5. Bind wall hanging as indicated in project instructions, treating the hanging sleeve as part of the backing.
6. Blindstitch bottom of hanging sleeve in place, taking care not to stitch through to front of quilt.
7. Insert dowel or slat into hanging sleeve.

SIGNING AND DATING YOUR QUILT

Your completed quilt is a work of art and should be treated as such. And like any artist, you should sign and date your work. There are many different ways to do this, and you should pick a method of signing and dating that reflects the quilt, the occasion for which it was made, and your own particular talents.

The following suggestions may give you an idea for recording the history of your quilt for future generations.

• Embroider your name, date, and any additional information on the quilt top or backing. You may use floss colors that closely match the fabric you are working on, such as white floss on a white border, or contrasting colors may be used.
• Make a label from muslin and use a permanent marker to write your information. Your label may be as plain or as fancy as you wish. Then stitch the label to the back of the quilt.
• Chart a cross-stitch label design that includes the information you wish and stitch it in colors that complement the quilt. Stitch the finished label to the quilt backing.

PILLOW FINISHING

Any quilt block may be made into a pillow. If desired, you may add welting to the pillow top before adding the backing.

MAKING THE PILLOW

1. For pillow back, cut a piece of fabric the same size as pieced and quilted pillow top.
2. Add welting to pillow top if indicated in project instructions (see below).
3. Place pillow back and pillow top right sides together. Using a 1/2" seam allowance (or stitching as close as possible to welting), sew pillow top and back together, leaving an opening at bottom edge for turning. Turn pillow right side out, carefully pushing corners outward. Stuff with polyester fiberfill or pillow form and sew final closure by hand.

ADDING WELTING

1. To make welting, measure outer dimensions of pillow top and add 2". Cut a bias strip of fabric the width specified in project instructions, equal in length to determined measurement, piecing if necessary.
2. Lay cord along center of bias strip on wrong side of fabric; fold strip over cord. Using a zipper foot, machine baste along length of strip close to cord. Trim seam allowance to 1/2".
3. Matching raw edges and beginning and ending 3" from ends of welting, baste welting to right side of pillow top. To make turning corners easier, clip seam allowance of welting at pillow top corners.
4. Remove approximately 3" of seam at 1 end of welting; fold fabric away from cord. Trim remaining end of welting so that cord ends meet exactly. Fold short edge of welting fabric 1/2" to wrong side; fold fabric back over area where ends meet (**Fig. 66**). Baste remainder of welting to pillow top close to cord.

Fig. 66

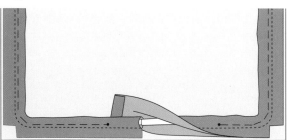

5. Follow Step 3 of **Making the Pillow** to complete pillow.

EMBROIDERY STITCHES

Blanket Stitch
Come up at 1. Go down at 2 and come up at 3, keeping thread below point of needle (**Fig. 67**). Continue working as shown in **Fig. 68**.

Fig. 67

Fig. 68

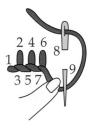

Chain Stitch
Come up at 1 and make a counterclockwise loop with the thread (**Fig. 69**). Go back down at 1 and come up at 2, keeping the thread below the point of the needle. Make a loop with the thread and go back down at 2; come up at 3, keeping thread below the point of the needle. Secure the last loop by bringing thread over loop and down (**Fig. 70**).

Fig. 69

Fig. 70

GLOSSARY

Appliqué — A cutout fabric shape that is secured to a larger background. Also refers to the technique of securing the cutout pieces.

Backing — The back or bottom layer of a quilt, sometimes called the "lining."

Backstitch — A reinforcing stitch taken at the beginning and end of a seam to secure stitches.

Basting — Large running stitches used to temporarily secure pieces or layers of fabric together. Basting is removed after permanent stitching.

Batting — The middle layer of a quilt; provides the insulation and warmth as well as the thickness.

Bias — The diagonal (45° for true bias) grain of fabric in relation to crosswise or lengthwise grain (see **Fig. 71**).

Binding — The fabric strip used to enclose the raw edges of the layered and quilted quilt. Also refers to the technique of finishing quilt edges in this way.

Border — Strips of fabric that are used to frame a quilt top.

Chain piecing — A machine-piecing method consisting of joining pairs of pieces one after the other by feeding them through the sewing machine without cutting the thread between the pairs.

Grain — The direction of the threads in woven fabric. "Crosswise grain" refers to the threads running from selvage to selvage. "Lengthwise grain" refers to the threads running parallel to the selvages (**Fig. 71**).

Fig. 71

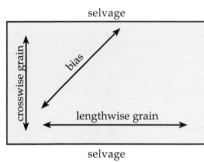

Machine baste — To baste using a sewing machine set at a long stitch length.

Miter — A method used to finish corners of quilt borders or bindings, consisting of joining fabric pieces at a 45° angle.

Piecing — Sewing together the pieces of a quilt design to form a quilt block or an entire quilt top.

Quilt block — Pieced or appliquéd sections that are sewn together to form a quilt top.

Quilt top — The decorative part of a quilt that is layered on top of the batting and backing.

Quilting — The stitching that holds together the 3 quilt layers (top, batting, and backing); or, the entire process of making a quilt.

Running stitch — A series of straight stitches with the stitch length equal to the space between stitches (**Fig. 72**).

Fig. 72

Sashing — Strips or blocks of fabric that separate individual blocks in a quilt top.

Seam allowance — The distance between the seam and the cut edge of the fabric. In quilting, this is usually 1/4".

Selvages — The 2 finished lengthwise edges of fabric (see **Fig. 71**). Selvages should be trimmed from fabric before cutting.

Set (or Setting) — The arrangement of the quilt blocks as they are sewn together to form the quilt top.

Setting squares — Squares of plain (unpieced) fabric set between pieced or appliquéd quilt blocks in a quilt top.

Setting triangles — Triangles of fabric used around the outside of a diagonally-set quilt top to fill in between outer squares and border or binding.

Stencil — A pattern used for marking quilting lines.

Straight grain — The crosswise or lengthwise grain of fabric (see **Fig. 71**). The lengthwise grain has the least amount of stretch.

Strip set — Two or more strips of fabric that are sewn together along the long edges, and then cut apart across the width of the sewn strips to create smaller units.

Template — A pattern used for marking quilt pieces to be cut out.

Triangle-square — In piecing, 2 right triangles joined along their long sides to form a square with a diagonal seam (**Fig. 73**).

Fig. 73

Unit — A pieced section that is made as individual steps in the quilt construction process are completed. Units are usually combined to make blocks or other sections of the quilt top.

CREDITS

We want to extend a warm *thank you* to the generous people who allowed us to photograph our projects at their homes.

- *Ohio Star:* Carl and Monte Brunck
- *Zigzag Quilt:* Carl and Monte Brunck
- *Double Wedding Ring Collection:* Carol Clawson
- *Pineapple Quilt:* Dick and Joan Rechtin
- *Trip Around the World Collection:* Thomas and Janet Feurig
- *Spring Bouquet Collection*: Scott and Sharon Mosley
- *Ohio Rose:* Dr. and Mrs. Michael Grounds
- *Baby Bear Collection:* Carol Clawson
- *Patriotic Gem:* Carl and Monte Brunck
- *Paramount Star:* Carol Clawson
- *Triple Irish Chain:* Nancy Gunn Porter
- *Blue Cathedral:* Susan Wildung
- *Adirondack Collection:* Dr. Tony Johnson
- *Nine-Patch Chain:* Nancy Gunn Porter
- *Autumn Baskets:* Nancy Gunn Porter

We also thank the Arkansas Territorial Restoration, Little Rock, Arkansas, for allowing us to photograph our *Schoolhouse Collection* at the museum.

The following quilts are from the collection of Bryce and Donna Hamilton, Minneapolis, Minnesota: Double Wedding Ring, page 20; Pineapple, page 28; Ohio Rose, page 54; Paramount Star, page 78; and Triple Irish Chain, page 102.

The Double Wedding Ring Wall Hanging shown on page 22 was created by Katie Mast, Millersburg, Ohio.

We also want to thank Lori McClain for the use of her hatboxes, which appear on pages 42-46.

To Magna IV Color Imaging of Little Rock, Arkansas, we say thank you for the superb color reproduction and excellent pre-press preparation.

We especially want to thank photographers Mark Mathews, Larry Pennington, Karen Busick Shirey, and Ken West of Peerless Photography, Little Rock, Arkansas, and Jerry R. Davis of Jerry Davis Photography, Little Rock, Arkansas, for their time, patience, and excellent work.

We extend a sincere *thank you* to all the people who assisted in making and testing the projects in this book: Karen Call, Deborah B. Chance, Nora Faye Clift, Stephanie Fite, Patricia Galas, Judith H. Hassed, Judith M. Kline, Barbara Middleton, Gazelle Mode, Sherri Mode, Ruby Solida, Glenda Taylor; the members of the First Assembly of God Church Women's Ministry, Searcy, Arkansas: Frances Blackburn, Louella English, Wanda Fite, Nan Goode, Bonnie Gowan, Juanita Hodges, Minnie Hogan, Ida Johnson, Ruby Johnson, Richadeen Lewis, Velrie Louks, and Minnie Whitehurst; members of the Highland Valley United Methodist Church, Little Rock, Arkansas: Frieda Bard, Thelma Bouton, Blanche Hicks, Jean Hooper, Joyce May, Ethil Martin, Velma Shaneyfelt, Lucile Shivley, and Ida Marie Sisco; and members of the Gardner Memorial United Methodist Church, North Little Rock, Arkansas: Elois Allain, Maxie Bramblett, Alice Dong, Vina Lendermon, Fredda McBride, Betty Smith, Esther Starkey, and Thelma Starkey.